ALL ABOUT YOUR CAR

by

David Kline and Jamie Robertson

D1605659

DIMI PRESS   Salem, Oregon

DIMI PRESS
3820 Oak Hollow Lane, SE
Salem, Oregon 97302-4774

© 1997 David N.Kline

This book is a work of advice and opinion. Neither the authors or the publisher are responsible for actions based on the contents of this book.

Retail price - $16.95, First Edition
10 9 8 7 6 5 4 3 2 1

Library of Congress Cataloging In Publication Data
  Kline, David Nigel, 1950-
    All about your car/by David Kline and Jamie Robertson.--1st ed.
        p. cm.
    Includes index.
    ISBN: 0-931625-32-7(pbk.)
    1. Automobiles--Maintenance and repair.
      I. Robertson, Jamie,1957- . II. Title.
    TL152.K573 1996
    629.28'72--dc20   96-35328
                                                 CIP

Cover design by Bruce DeRoos
Illustrations by O.C. Dobrostanski
Printed in 12 pt. Palatino

TABLE OF CONTENTS

PART II - MAINTAINING YOUR CAR

How the proper basic maintenance on a car can prevent up to 80% or more of all mechanical breakdowns from occurring.

Breaking in a new car. Handling older cars

This chapter covers the maintenance on fluids (oil, water, etc., when and how to check them, when to add, what to add, what not to add, when to change the fluids. This includes graphics showing where these fluid systems are located). Also covered are checking tires, brakes, steering, tune-ups etc., items that if not checked can cause safety problems or lead to mechanical complications.

This chapter covers the basic simple repairs that can be done by just about anyone, covering some of the basic tools and how to handle them.

Included are:

- What to include in a basic tool and emergency kit
- How to properly jump start a car
- How to clean off battery terminals
- How to change a battery
- How to change a tire
- How to do an oil change
- How to flush out a radiator

Highlights of the main problems that can go wrong with an automobile.

PART III - BUYING YOUR CAR

What to consider, what to look for and what to ask when buying a car. This chapter includes a comprehensive checklist for you to use that should weed out the lemons and result in a good deal.

PART IV - GETTING YOUR CAR FIXED

How can you find a good mechanic, and how can you get the most out of them once you find them?

How you can help the mechanic to diagnose the problem.

How the customer can be responsible for how well the car runs and how he will be treated by the mechanic.

This section contains various tricks that have actually been used by unscrupulous mechanics to simulate problems that didn't really exist, and charge the customer for the repair.

- Simple tests you can use to see if you are being tricked in this way.
- Two key rules to preventing rip-offs.

With the "Repair Checklist" when a mechanic says "you need a new _____", you can look up the symptoms of such a part being broken and cross check these against the symptoms you are experiencing with your car.

This glossary contains simple definitions of many of the key terms that you will come across on the subject of cars. This is not meant to be a complete automotive dictionary but should help to keep you from falling asleep when your mechanic starts talking.

Index

Trouble Shooting Checklist

This is designed as a separate booklet (to be placed in your glove compartment) and tells you how to determine what is causing the symptom; what to look for, and what to listen for. Then suggests possible repairs.

INTRODUCTION

This book is intended to give a basic understanding in layman's terms, without requiring a degree in automotive engineering, of how your car works, what can go wrong with it, and how to judge what needs to be done to get your car back on it's feet, up and running. Apply the information in this book and we are confident you will save a great deal of time, money, and frayed nerves.

We have not tried, by any stretch of the imagination, to cover everything there is to know about cars. We are not trying to make a professional mechanic of you. Our intention is to provide a basic comprehension of this modern wonder in a way that you will understand. This book will provide practical assistance in the handling of automobile problems.

Perhaps you have had the unfortunate experience of encountering technical writers who forget that those who are reading the book probably do NOT have the same knowledge that they do. Consequently the product is nearly incomprehensible to all but scholars in the field. Technical subjects do not have to be written in this way. Obviously, all of us have some degree of knowledge about cars already, but most of us have not been properly educated in this subject. Since the degree of each reader's knowledge is going to be different we have attempted here to cover all bases. The information is presented in the simplest and most basic style possible, without making any assumptions of what you might or might not know.

We hope we have produced a book that is interesting, enjoyable, and informative. You, the reader, will have to be the judge of whether we have succeeded.

We are concerned in this book with presenting a basic understanding of how cars work. Therefore the text and illustrations that are presented will cover these basics. Brand new and recent model cars may include sophistications that are not in themselves pertinent to the basic operation of cars, and indeed to attempt to cover these would create a diversion from our purpose and a distraction from your comprehension. So when you open up the hood of your new car it may not look entirely like our illustrations, and our purposefully simple descriptions may lack some of the modern advances and sophistications that have been engineered into your automobile. Rest assured that in its basic structure and function your car operates as described and it is a knowledge of these basics that is vital to your understanding of, and to an excellent relationship with, your car.

David Kline
Jamie Robertson

PART 1- HOW YOUR CAR WORKS

CHAPTER 1. THE BASICS OF HOW CARS WORK

An automobile is a moving vehicle. Literally it "moves itself", or creates its own motion rather than being pushed by physical force. In other words we don't sit in it and push with our feet!

An engine is literally "something that produces." In a car an engine produces mechanical power that is then converted into motion (mechanical just means "performed by a machine").

An automobile comes with an engine, or motor, which burns fuel to create heat and pressure. The engine is called an "internal combustion" engine, which means literally that it creates a fire and burns fuel inside the engine. ("internal" = inside; "combustion" = action of burning). The heat and pressure is then converted into a type of energy or power and is utilized in such a way that it makes the wheels of the vehicle turn, and so causes the vehicle to move forwards or backwards.

As an analogy, let's take the example of the human body:

1. We eat food;

2. We convert the food by digesting it;

A SIMPLE MOTOR

KEY

CLOCKWISE MOTION WINDS KEY UP

ANTICLOCKWISE MOTION, WHEN KEY IS RELEASED,
RESULTS IN FORWARD MOTION OF THE TOY CAR

3. The food is converted to fuel and enters the blood stream;

4. The fuel is transferred as needed to the nerves and the muscles;

5. When we give the command, the muscles of the legs will move the legs forward (or backwards) and we either walk or run, using the fuel to create power.

A motor vehicle is really an extension of our legs, as it simply allows us to move faster than our legs will carry us. The car operates in a similar way to the points in the body that are listed above. We are going to take a look at the mouth, digestive system, blood stream, nerves, backbone, muscles, legs, and so forth, of a car and see how they work together to give the car forward or backward motion.

A Simple Motor

Before we look at a complex automobile motor, let us look at a very simple type of motor, so that we can understand the basic concept of what a motor is, what it does, and how it does it: The picture opposite shows a motor for a toy car.

A motor by definition is something that creates motion. In the example shown in the picture we have a key that gets wound up tightly, which tightens a spring. The spring attaches to the wheels of the car.

When the key is let go and the car is placed on the ground on its wheels the force that was wound up into the spring is released. This released force moves the wheels and the toy car moves forward.

It will move forward until the tension in the spring winds down; that is, until it runs out of force or power, or until it runs into an object such as a wall and is stopped.

So the most basic concept of a motor is that power (which is defined as "potential motion") is created, and this power is then released and converted into actual motion. This, in its basic concept, is what happens with a real car (though hopefully it does not get driven into a wall). The difference between a toy car and a real car is simply:

1. How the power is generated,

2. How the power is released,

3. How long the power will last.

Look around your house. Identify a few items that operate with motors.

The Main Systems

Let's get an overview of the main systems that together make up a car that will start, move (hopefully where you want it to go) and stop (hopefully when you want it to).

1. **The starter/ignition system** gets the car started. It gets the engine to turn over; and the distributor sending electricity to the spark plugs.

2. **The fuel system** delivers the fuel to the the engine. The fuel is pumped from the fuel tank via filters to the carburetor or fuel injection system and into the cylinders for combustion.

3. **The engine** takes in the fuel, explodes it, and sends the power generated to the transmission so the car can move forward.

4. **The lubrication system** keeps the moving parts of the engine lubricated so they operate smoothly despite the heat and friction.

5. **The cooling system** keeps the engine cool so it doesn't overheat.

6. **The transmission or gear-box** takes the power from the engine and transmits it to the wheels for forward or backward drive.

7. **The exhaust system** gets rid of the poisonous waste from the combustion process.

8. **The steering system** enables the driver to direct where the car will go.

9. **The braking system** enables the driver to stop the car or slow it down as needed.

10. **The suspension system** protects car and riders from the roughness of the road.

11. **The electrical system** keeps the electrical power flowing where it is needed in the car.

12. **The chassis or frame** holds the whole machine together and provides the framework on which to build the interior of the car.

13. **The interior** gives the driver, who is the primary mind and brain of the vehicle, a place to sit and direct. It also provides the driver with the information and controls he needs to run the vehicle.

Remember that these individual systems are carefully coordinated into a functioning whole. The timing of this coordination and the interaction between the systems is every bit as important as the individual systems themselves. In this way the energy is generated, magnified, converted, and passed on smoothly from one point to another and the car operates as an efficient, safe, and comfortable mode of transportation.

The Parts of the Machine

Today's motor car contains thousands of parts. Trying to understand a machine with this many parts can be rather overwhelming. Remember that an automobile motor is simply a machine that creates, magnifies, and utilizes energy or power for the purpose of moving a vehicle forwards or backwards. All these thousands of parts have this purpose in common.

Continuing our analogy, a human body has hundreds of parts itself. However, if you break the body down into its basic components, it consists of organs, bones, muscles, skin, blood, nerves and so on. If you had a clear understanding of these key components, what they do and how they do it, then the complexity of the body would start to make sense.

A mind receives information, stores information and thinks with that information to make decisions. In a car you, the driver, are the vehicle's mind, possibly aided to some degree by the instrument panel or an on-board computer. The brain in your skull is a switch-board that translates those decisions into impulses that drive and coordinate the body. In a car, this brain is you, aided by the computer if you have one. The electrical system in the car sends electrical impulses through the car rather like the nervous system sends nerve impulses around the body.

The motor has its own mouth, a set of "lungs" and a "stomach", breathing in the air and digesting and using the "food." Various filters in the car act like the liver and kidneys in the body cleansing the machine of impurities. The engine is like the heart and keeps the life pumping into the machine. The transmission could be considered the backbone. The wheels and tires are the legs and feet.

With the car turned off and the brakes set, inspect your car inside and outside, and then open up the hood to your car. Compare what you see to the large diagram. Note which of the items in the drawing you can identify in your car. Touch the various parts of the car. With the engine off, of course!

Now turn the engine on and spend a few minutes listening to the different sounds and watching what is happening under the hood. Touch nothing under the hood while the engine is running!

Some Mechanical Parts

Certain mechanical ("performed by a machine") parts are vital to the running and coordination of a car. They let fluids flow, or prevent fluids from escaping. They push onto or into other mechanisms to make them work, or they pull other things along. They take power and transfer it, or they magnify the power received and send it on. In reality there are just a few basic types of mechanical parts that occur many, many times in different forms, shapes, and sizes with different functions. It will make an understanding of cars a lot easier if they are familiar to you.

- A **switch** turns the power (usually electrical) on and off to a component. It opens up or closes off a flow of energy from one point to another.

- A **hose** carries fluid or air from one place to another.

- A **spring** holds tension and releases tension.

- A **seal** prevents a liquid from escaping from a specific area where it is needed; or prevents unwanted oil, water, or other substances from entering an area where they are not wanted.

- A **pump** creates constant pressure to move fluid to where it is needed.

- A **valve** is like a door which opens and shuts to let fluids or gases pass in or out.

- A **piston** is a plunger that moves up and down and pushes some other part (like a shaft) in the process.

- A **shaft** is a long piece of connecting metal often attached to a piston at one end and usually a gear at the other. It transfers power between two points as it turns.

• A **gear** is a disc, roller, or shaft with teeth. One gear connects to another gear of smaller or larger size by having teeth of the same size that fit into one another (called intermeshing). Smaller gears have fewer teeth and larger gears have more teeth. A gear may be attached to and receive power from, or transfer power to, a shaft.

• A **bearing** is a lubricated component connecting a shaft and another mechanical part that allows the shaft to turn with greater ease.

• A **pulley** is a round disc with a groove in it for holding or gripping a belt. The pulley moves in a circle and it either drives or is driven by a belt.

• A **belt** connects two or more pulleys, being turned by one of them and in turn driving the other.

4. The solenoid lets the electricity through to the starter motor.

5. The starter motor, by turning a gear at the back of the engine, gives the engine a quick and sudden burst of power that gets the engine running.

Now go to your car and see if you can locate the solenoid, the starter motor, the battery, and the engine. Turn on the car. Can you hear the pistons going up and down? (If you can't find these things, get a friend who is familiar with automobile engines to help you).

Chapter 3. The Ignition System

Simultaneously, when the key is turned on, the electrical power from the battery is connected up to the distributor.

The electricity reaches the distributor after passing through a special coil that causes surges of sufficient electrical pressure to create sparks. All the distributor does is distribute the electricity it receives to the engine. Specifically it distributes tiny electrical pulses to each of the spark plugs at the right intervals. The spark plugs are literally just that— they are small plugs that create the spark that will ignite the fuel to be burned in the engine.

These days many cars have an electronic ignition system. This carries out the same functions as the distributor but it is all done by a computerized electronic chip. The mechanisms are a little different but the principles are similar.

The mechanical motion of the engine has been set into play by the starter motor. This causes the pistons in the engine to go up and down. The pistons are like plungers that fit inside the round cylinders in the engine. As the piston moves down it pulls in the fuel and air. The spark from the spark plugs causes the fuel and air mixture to explode, creating heat and pressure and this produces power in the engine. Let's recap that:

1. The key is turned on.

2. The starter motor puts the engine into motion, while electricity goes from the battery via the coil to the distributor.

3. This distributes an electrical flow to each of the spark plugs.

4. The pistons move down and pull in fuel and air, through the intake valve.

5. The spark from the spark plugs ignites the fuel mixture which explodes, creating heat and pressure resulting in power.

With the engine off and cooled off, look under the hood and touch the spark plugs, and the distributor or electronic ignition.

NOTE: Be sure that the engine is completely cooled off before touching the spark plugs, or any other part of the engine block! Various parts of the motor typically attain extremely high temperatures while the car is running, and these parts can take a little while to cool off after turning off the motor.

200 HORSEPOWER

Chapter 4. The Electrical System

The electrical system starts with the battery. A battery is simply a power pack that generates electricity.

Any flow involves pressure. For example, water flows out of a tap with a certain amount of pressure. The pressure of an electrical flow is measured in what is called volts.

A battery that puts out 12 volts just means more electricity than, say, a battery that puts out 9 volts.

The initial jolt of power to a car starts with an electric battery consisting of 12 volts. As a comparison, an "AAA" size battery used, for example, in small tape recorders has 1.5 volts. A "D" size battery used to power slightly larger equipment has 9 volts.

Today's motor car creates several hundred horse power of energy. One horse power is equivalent to the power which one horse would use to pull a vehicle. So a car with "200 horse power" has the equivalent potential pulling power of 200 horses running at full gallop. This power is generated by the engine and converted into motion by the transmission. But the engine creates its energy by burning fuel and to burn the fuel it requires a means to light the fuel. This function is provided by the battery. The battery is simply the fuse that sparks the firecracker inside the engine which creates energy which is harnessed by the transmission as the "horse power" of a moving car.

BATTERY FLOWS ENERGY

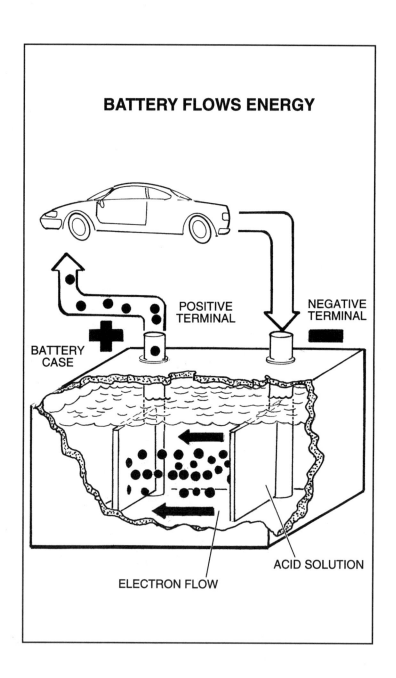

POSITIVE
TERMINAL

NEGATIVE
TERMINAL

BATTERY
CASE

ACID SOLUTION

ELECTRON FLOW

How the battery works

Two plates made from different types of metal are placed in an acid solution. Due to the nature of the metals, when they come into contact with the acid there is a chemical reaction.

As a result of this reaction electricity is released. Electricity is a flow of electrons. Electrons are simply particles that contain a type of energy (or electrical charge) that has been named "negative charge." This is just an agreed upon name. This type of electrical energy flow is used for a multitude of household and industrial purposes, running lights, machinery, and so forth.

The battery in your car has two posts that stick up. These are known as terminals, a terminal being something that receives or relays a flow (in this case a flow of electrons). The terminals are connected to the plates. The "negative" plate then is the one that the electrons move away from during the chemical process taking place in the battery. The "positive" plate is the one the electrons move to during the chemical process. With the chemical reaction electrons travel inside the battery from the "negative" to the "positive" terminal. They build up on the "positive" terminal.

These electrons are then released from the positive terminal out into the car by cables and wire.

The circuit (a complete electrical flow) between the "positive" and "negative" terminals is then completed outside of the battery, in the car itself.

THE ALTERNATOR

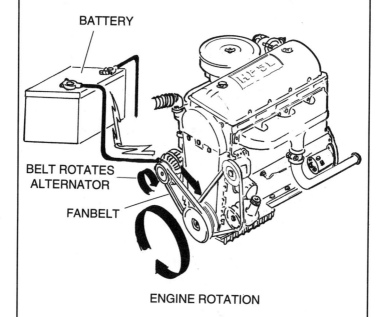

BATTERY

BELT ROTATES
ALTERNATOR

FANBELT

ENGINE ROTATION

Let's take that again point by point:

1. Two different plates in the battery are placed in an acid solution.

2. The chemicals react.

3. Electrons move from away from the "negative" plate to the "positive" plate.

4. The circuit is completed on the outside of the battery.

The Alternator

When the battery sends electrons out into the car, it is actually discharging itself. The battery is getting rid of its own power by this process.

Luckily, the 12 volt battery in the car is rechargeable. It is recharged by the alternator. The alternator contains a magnet that is capable of receiving mechanical force from the engine and converting it back into electrical force, creating a new flow of electrons. The alternator directs and forces these electrons back to the battery so that the battery can re-charge itself. In this respect the alternator is functioning as a generator, or more accurately re-generating the flow of electricity, which is called a current.

The introduction of these electrons back into the battery reverses the chemical reaction that occurred when the battery generated the electricity in the first place. This brings it back to square one and the whole process begins again.

When a battery goes dead the continuous circuit of electrical flow from the battery, out to the car and back through the alternator, has broken down. It can break down within the battery, in the alternator, or due to an electrical malfunction somewhere in the car.

The effect in any of these cases is that the chemical reaction ceases to occur in the battery. Sometimes you will be able to get the battery recharged if it goes dead. However for various reasons the battery may break down and no longer be rechargeable and must be replaced. This can be checked using equipment that your mechanic has.

An additional function of the alternator is as a "regulator", literally regulating the flow of electricity. It ensures that a steady current is sent to the various electrical components, and that this current does not get too strong. Too much current will damage the electrical components. It also regulates the amount of current going back into the battery, as overcharging the battery with too much current will destroy it as surely as letting it discharge.

The Electrical Flow

You won't get too far without a properly working electrical system! The electrical system of the car provides the flow of electricity to all those points in the car that need electricity to function. As we have seen the battery provides the power to start the starter. It also provides the power to the distributor that is then sent to the spark plugs, creating the spark that enables the combustion process to occur in the engine cylinder.

Electricity is also used in a car to enable the following parts to operate:

1. The **fuel pump**. (On some cars this is mechanical, not electrical).

2. The **computer** in a fuel injection system, or the on-board computer if the car has one.

3. The **instrument panel**, informing the driver of how the car is running.

4. The **side lights**, the **head lights**, the **reversing lights**, the **indicator lights**, the **hazard lights**, the **interior lights**.

5. The **horn**.

6. The **radio**.

7. The **cigarette lighter**, which can also be used as a power supply for other accessories.

8. The **air conditioning**.

Each of the parts supplied with electricity is also supplied with a fuse. A fuse is an electrical safety device, containing a metal wire or strip. When a flow of electricity through the fuse becomes too strong, the fuse melts, interrupting the circuit and preventing damage to the electrical machinery involved. The fuse box containing these fuses is usually located under the front dash board by the driver's seat. The electric current is carried by wires to the various points where it will be used. These wires are normally well protected and will not cause trouble.

Look under the hood again and see how the battery is hooked up to the alternator.

Track down some of the wires and see where they go.

THE ELECTRICAL FLOW

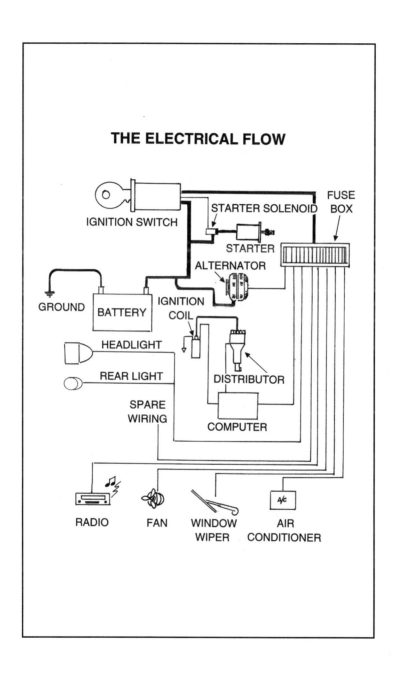

CHAPTER 5. THE FUEL SYSTEM

Most cars use some form of gasoline, known as "gas", as a fuel. Gasoline is derived from petroleum, a dark, oily, flammable liquid found in the earth's crust. Usually modern cars use only unleaded gasoline which is better for the environment. Older cars may use leaded gasoline. Some cars are designed to operate off diesel or other fuels. Use only the correct type of fuel for your car. This will usually be marked next to the opening at the top of your fuel tank, and it will certainly be stated clearly in the manual for your car.

Gasoline is a liquid form of a gas. It can easily be turned into a gas vapor and it will burn easily if mixed with air (oxygen) and when coming into contact with any type of open flame or spark. This is why you must keep any open flame, lighter, cigarette, etc., away from your gas tank or engine.

Do not ever use any kind of flame near your gas tank or a running engine. Never use a match or lighter to look under the hood of your car at night. Gas leaks can occur in a car and leak out gas in a vaporized form. You cannot see it, but it will explode upon contact with any kind of open flame.

A car engine is designed to create a safe, controlled fire to produce heat and pressure, resulting in a release of energy or power which is then harnessed to create motion.

WARNING - DO NOT EVER HAVE AN OPEN FLAME, MATCH OR LIGHTER OR A LIT CIGA-RETTE ANYWHERE NEARBY WHEN LOOKING AT OR WORKING UNDER YOUR HOOD, OR WHEN FILLING YOUR GAS TANK

The Fuel Flow

The gasoline (or "gas") is filled into and stored in a tank, usually away from the engine so as to prevent sparks from the engine reaching and get-ting into the gas tank. When your car is running, the fuel is carried from the gas tank through a fuel line, which is a tube connected at one end to the gas tank and at the other end to the motor. There is a system of filters to catch any impurities in the gasoline. A pick-up pipe, usually with a filter in the bottom, car-ries the fuel to a fuel pump that pushes out the fuel through another fuel filter and then to the carbure-tor (or the fuel injection system).

Cars have either a carburetor or a fuel injec-tion system and we will explain both of these. Es-sentially they do the same job of distributing the fuel to the engine, they just accomplish it in slightly dif-ferent ways. The fuel injection system requires a much more powerful fuel pump than a carburetor. The right pump must be used in either case. If a car-buretor pump is used for a fuel injection system it will not be powerful enough to do the job. If a fuel injection pump is used for a carburetor it will flood the carburetor with too much fuel and prevent the engine from working properly.

Let's Review:

1. The gasoline is stored in the gas tank.

2. The gas is pulled by the fuel pump through the fuel filter to clean it and passed to the carburetor or fuel injection system.

3. The carburetor or fuel injection system regulates the flow of fuel and air to the engine.

Can you find the carburetor or the fuel injection system in your car? The carburetor is under the air cleaner. Take off the air cleaner and filter and look inside the carburetor if you have one. Feel the gasoline residue inside it.

The Carburetor

The fuel pump pushes fuel to the carburetor which has a small bowl that holds the fuel. Inside this bowl sits what is known as the float (a type of valve that floats in the fuel) and when the right amount of fuel is contained in the bowl the float or valve senses this and shuts off.

The engine contains a vacuum (absence of air). When the pistons inside this engine move downwards this vacuum pulls the fuel from the carburetor, taking it through a number of tiny jets into the engine. The jets are tiny holes which the fuel is forced through and the pressure of this action vaporizes the fuel.

This vaporized fuel mixes with air which has been pulled in by the same vacuum effect through the air filter, and the air valve, into the carburetor. The fuel and air mixture is then directed through the intake valves into the engine. The air contains oxygen which when mixed in the right proportions with the vaporized fuel will make a combustible material (meaning simply that it can be lit and made to easily catch on fire).

Okay:

1. The pistons in the engine move down.

2. The vacuum pulls the available fuel and air from the carburetor.

3. The fuel is pulled through tiny jets and is turned in to vapor.

4. The fuel/air mixture is pulled through the intake valve of the engine and is ready to be burned.

Fuel Injection

Most newer cars have fuel injection systems. A fuel injection system is computerized and continuously distributes the right amount of fuel to each of the engine cylinders, opening up the intake valves into the engine at the right time, and keeping up an exact pressure. Fuel injection is a superior form of

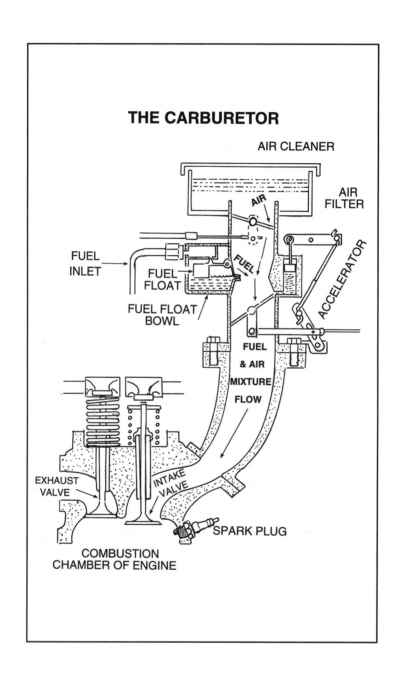

THE CARBURETOR

management and distribution of fuel to the engine than a carburetor. There is a system of sensors that tells the computer exactly what is occurring with the fuel intake, air intake, oxygen levels, fuel consumption rate, gas and poison levels in the exhaust system, and so forth. The computer can then make exact adjustments on the amount of fuel and air being let in to the engine. This results in a very efficient use of fuel and maximum engine efficiency.

If there is a problem with one of the sensors the computer will turn on a light to inform the driver of the problem. The computer will give a code stating exactly what needs to be fixed. It is unnecessary to replace the whole fuel injection system if just one part is faulty. A competent mechanic who knows fuel injection systems will know how to retrieve the code from the computer, determine the exact problem, and repair it without having to replace the entire fuel injection mechanism.

Not all mechanics have kept pace with technological advances such as fuel injection, however, and those that have not may try to take the easy way out, telling you that you have to replace the whole fuel injection system when this may not be the case.

1. The fuel injection system uses sensors to monitor the levels of fuel, air, exhaust, etc.

2. There is a computer that uses the data from these sensors to manage the distribution of fuel and air to the engine.

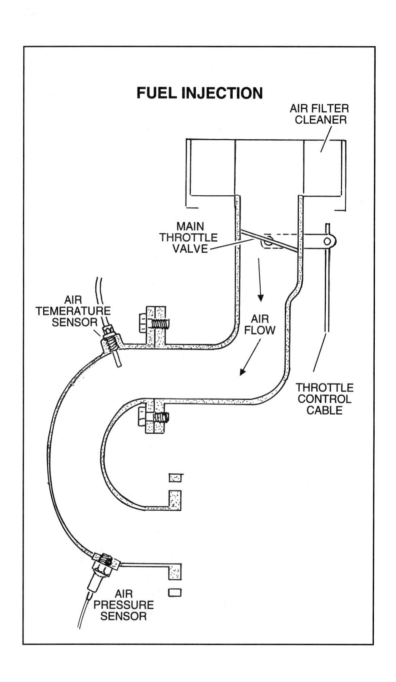

FUEL INJECTION

AIR FILTER
CLEANER

MAIN
THROTTLE
VALVE

AIR
TEMERATURE
SENSOR

AIR
FLOW

THROTTLE
CONTROL
CABLE

AIR
PRESSURE
SENSOR

3. The computer generates a code if there is a problem with the fuel injection system, telling the mechanic exactly what needs to be fixed.

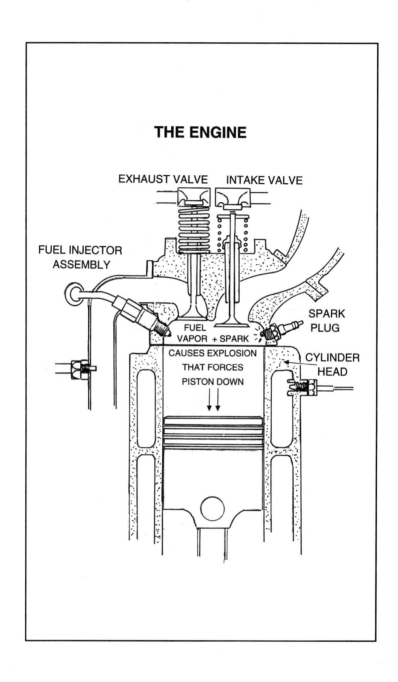

THE ENGINE

EXHAUST VALVE INTAKE VALVE

FUEL INJECTOR
ASSEMBLY

SPARK
PLUG

FUEL
VAPOR + SPARK
CAUSES EXPLOSION
THAT FORCES
PISTON DOWN

CYLINDER
HEAD

Chapter 6. The Engine

Burning the Fuel

As described in the section on the fuel system, the fuel is pulled into the engine. Let's see how this fuel is utilized:

The engine contains pistons. Pistons are really just a type of metal pump which move up and down. Each piston is encased in a steel sleeve, called a cylinder. The fuel/air mixture is let into the cylinder.

An explosion is caused when the spark from the spark plug comes into contact with the gas vapor and oxygen mixture that has been let into the cylinder. This explosion forces the piston down. This motion of the piston creates power which is then harnessed to produce the forward motion of the car.

The burning and exploding that takes place inside the engine is called "combustion". It occurs inside the engine or "internally". Thus, a motor car engine is called an "internal combustion engine." This combustion process creates a tremendous amount of friction, pressure, and heat reaching extremely high temperatures. Unless a cooling process takes place the parts of an engine would just fry and weld together. The engine has a jacket around it which is full of coolant which keeps the engine cool.

1. The spark from the spark plug touches the fuel/air mixture and ignites it.

2. The resulting explosion causes the piston to move up and down.

3. The motion of the piston produces power which is harnessed to make the car move.

4. A cooling system keeps the heat from melting the engine.

If you get a chance, see if your mechanic has a car on which he is performing engine work. Ask if he will let you come and take a look at the inside of the engine.

The Basic "Four-Stroke" Engine

The explosion cycle that takes place in the engine has four stages or strokes and the pistons go through these four stages repetitively, at very high speed. The four stroke cycle takes place within each individual cylinder.

Stroke #1: Intake
As the piston moves down, the intake valve opens and lets in the fuel / air mixture.

Stroke #2: Compression
The piston moves back up and compresses the gas mixture.

Stroke #3: Power

> The compressed gas is ignited by the spark from the spark plug. The gas explodes and pushes the piston back down generating the power which is harnessed to drive the car.

Stroke #4: Exhaust

> The piston returns upwards, opening the exhaust valve and letting the exhausted burned gas out into the exhaust system.

The power is harnessed in stroke #3. As the explosion takes place the piston pushes one of the major components of the car. This is the crankshaft. This is the shaft that connects and transfers power from the engine to the transmission.

The piston attaches to the crankshaft by means of a connecting rod. The piston, rod, and crankshaft are joined together in a way that causes the crankshaft to revolve at high speed.

The entire purpose of all the prior actions that have taken place in the car, the battery, the starter, the spark from the spark plugs, the fuel and air from the carburetor, the four-strokes of the engine is to make this crankshaft move.

The four-stroke cycle takes place within each combustion chamber. Your car has several cylinders (usually four or more). The different cylinders are lined up to perform the four stroke cycle one after the other in a specific, precisely timed sequence. This sequence can vary slightly depending on the number of cylinders and the make of car. The four-stroke cycle within any one cylinder always occurs in the sequence of strokes outlined above.

All Together Now: "Timing"

Now we get to the heart of the matter. In the body there is a vital coordination between air coming in to the lungs through the mouth or the nose, the assimilation of this oxygen into the blood stream (followed by the expulsion of the leftover gases back out through the lungs), and the pumping motion of the heart, carrying the blood to the vital organs. Similarly, several activities in the engine must be exactly coordinated and in a car this must be done precisely in time:

1. The **distributor** sends a jolt to each spark plug at the exact right time causing the spark to enter each combustion chamber at the right moment.

2. The **intake valve** to that chamber opens at the exact right time to let in the fuel/air mixture, in coordination with the timing of the spark

3. The **piston** to that chamber moves back up to compress the gas, timed to coordinate with the spark and the intake of the fuel/air mixture, so it can be ignited.

"Timing" is the relationship in time between the spark, the opening of the intake valve, and the

TIMING BELT

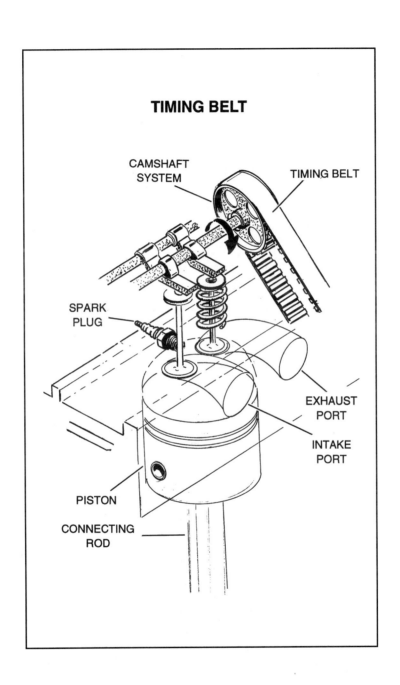

CAMSHAFT
SYSTEM

TIMING BELT

SPARK
PLUG

EXHAUST
PORT

INTAKE
PORT

PISTON

CONNECTING
ROD

compression stroke of the pistons. A correctly timed relationship between the spark reaching the combustion chamber, the valves opening to let in gas and the pistons moving up, compressing and then exploding the gas, will result in smooth, efficient running of the engine.

This concept of timing is probably the single most important, fundamental factor to understand regarding the workings of a car engine. If you fully understand this you will understand the major problems that can occur with an engine and it will become very clear what to look for when a car is running poorly. It will often be something that is causing a problem in the coordination of this timing.

On the next few pages we are going to explore this in some detail. It may look complex, but the whole subject of cars will become much simpler if you take the time and effort to comprehend this. Make some diagrams of your own on this and go over the sequence a few times until it becomes clear.

Lucky is he whose mechanic fully understands this concept, can correctly set up the timing, and knows how to correct it when it goes wrong. This mechanic will be able to correctly diagnose your car!

How is this timing coordinated?

    1. There is a belt (rubber) or a chain (metal) that is attached to two pulleys. These pulleys

attach to the engine. The belt (or chain) connects the camshaft and the crankshaft.

2. Each pulley comes marked. The top pulley is connected to the camshaft and the mark on this pulley lines up to a mark on the camshaft. The bottom pulley is connected to the crankshaft and similarly a mark on this pulley lines up with a mark on the crankshaft.

3. When these marks are all lined up exactly then piston #1 will be sitting at its highest possible point in the cylinder. This position is known as "Top Dead Center" or "TDC". The timing belt or timing chain is placed around the pulley, with these marks lined up.

4. The distributor is connected to this set-up. As the camshaft/crankshaft pulley system turns it will rotate a part of the distributor called the rotor.

5. The distributor contains a rotor that rotates to distribute the spark to each piston in turn. There is also a mark on the rotor. The distributor cap houses the electrical contacts which create the spark that then goes to the spark plugs. Each piston has its own point of electrical contact. The rotor is set so that it is a slight, precise distance in front of the contact point for piston #1.

6. The reason for setting it this way, slightly in front of the electrical contact, is that before the spark is sent into the cylinder, the first down stroke of the piston must occur. This will cause the camshaft to open the intake valve and let the fuel/air mixture into the combustion chamber. Now the spark can be sent via the spark plug to piston #1 to ignite the fuel.

So the overall sequence is:

a) the crankshaft moves, pushing the piston down

b) the crankshaft pulley moves, pulling the timing belt,

c) the timing belt pulls the camshaft pulley,

d) the camshaft moves,

e) the intake valve opens,

f) the fuel enters the combustion chamber,

g) the piston moves back up to compress the fuel,

h) meanwhile the gear connected to the distributor rotor has begun moving the rotor into position, and

i) just as the piston comes back up, the rotor reaches the "point" for piston #1. The spark is created and sent via the spark plug into the combustion chamber to ignite the fuel.

Explosion!

The key to this sequence of actions occurring correctly, each action at its precise time, is that the marks on the pulleys and the rotor are lined up by the mechanic in the correct position.

The Accelerator

When you put your foot down on the accelerator all you are doing is opening the carburetor valve or the fuel injection valve to let more of the air / fuel mixture through into the engine. This valve is called the throttle.

More fuel gets burned and this increases the speed at which the engine turns (which is called increasing the engine "revs" or revolutions per minute). It is rather similar to the fact that a man who is running will breathe faster, the faster he runs.

Engine "Revs"

So what is it that is actually "revolving"? What are RPMs? It is the rotations per minute of the crankshaft.

ACCELERATOR PEDAL CONTROLS

CARBURETOR
OR
FUEL INJECTOR

CABLE
LINKAGE

FOOT PEDAL

Most cars have a dial that shows the RPMs or revolutions per minute also known as "revs." This dial is called a tachometer or "tach" (pronounced "tack"). The numbers on the dial are in thousands of revolutions per minute.

The "tach" in most cars when they are coasting in gear should sit at around two and a half to three on the dial. This will get the best miles per gallon out of your car and result in the least wear and tear on the engine. Consistently driven at higher "revs" your car will start to guzzle gas. You should shift up from one gear to the next when the "tach" hits about three and a half on the dial. And shift down to the next lower gear when the "tach" goes much below two and a half.

Do not push the "revs" above the red line marked on the tachometer. If you go over the maximum level of RPMs that is safe for your car as shown by the red line the engine valves will be permanently damaged. The engine will "fire" while the valves are still open and the car will backfire. For normal driving purposes you do not need to get anywhere near the red line on the dial, even when accelerating or overtaking.

With the car parked and the engine running, lift up the hood of your car, and leave the car door open. Put your foot on the accelerator with the hand brake on and the car out of gear. Gently increase the pressure on the gas pedal. Listen to the engine. Do you hear the increase in revs? Don't rev it too high!

How The Engine Connects to the Transmission

The piston connects to the rod.

The rod is connected to the crankshaft.

The crank is connected to a flywheel (a type of gear) that is connected to a clutch.

The clutch is connected to the gear-box or transmission.

The gearbox connects via the drive shaft to the differential. The differential is just another type of gear that transfers the right amount of power to each of the wheels.

The differential controls the axles. The axles are the connectors between the wheels.

The piston moves the rod, which moves the crankshaft, which moves the flywheel, which (via the clutch and gear-box) moves the drive shaft, which moves the differential, which moves the axles.

The axles turn the wheels.

The car moves.

Voila!

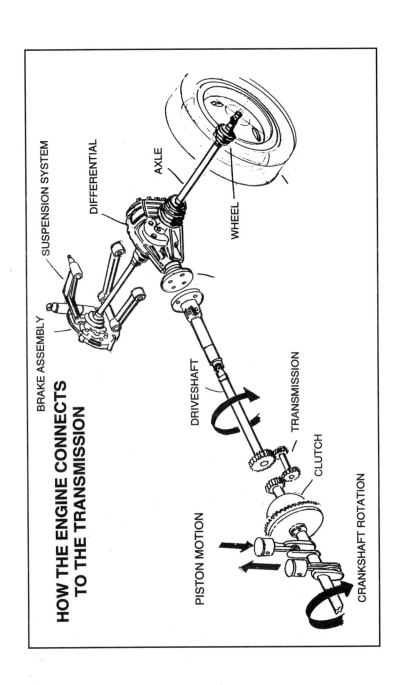

HOW THE ENGINE CONNECTS TO THE TRANSMISSION

BRAKE ASSEMBLY

SUSPENSION SYSTEM

DIFFERENTIAL

AXLE

WHEEL

DRIVESHAFT

TRANSMISSION

CLUTCH

PISTON MOTION

CRANKSHAFT ROTATION

Chapter 7. The Cooling System

We have clearly noted the importance of keeping the engine cooled off. Now we will explain how this is done.

Coolant (Anti-freeze) vs. water

Coolant is liquid that maintains a constant temperature and will neither heat up too high nor get too cold and freeze. It is stored in the radiator. Many people use a mixture of water and coolant and some only water. We recommend using coolant only as water will rust the inside of your engine (which is made of cast iron), causing deterioration in the engine itself and putting rust into the entire cooling system. Only use water in an emergency, such as a leak, so you are not stuck on the roadside. Then flush out your radiator immediately and replace the water with pure coolant, after any appropriate repairs.

The circulation of the coolant in the cooling system is generated by the water pump. This is a mechanical pump with propellers inside that are turned by a belt. This belt moves because it is connected to a moving pulley of the engine. As the engine turns over the belt moves and the water pump operates. The pump forces the water out of the engine and to the thermostat. The thermostat is just a temperature sensor that controls a valve. At a temperature of about 180 degrees the thermostat valve lets the hot water from the engine move into the radiator. As the hot water moves into the radiator this pushes cooler water out of the radiator and back into the engine. The hot fluid that has entered the radiator is now cooled down, due to the forward motion of the car causing cooler outside air to hit the radiator, usually assisted by a radiator fan. This whole cooling system circuit must be clear of barriers, stoppages, and leaks to work efficiently.

If your car does start to overheat, stop immediately, repeat IMMEDIATELY. Do not drive on even for a minute to try to get to a gas station. Just stop now. Let the car cool off. Then you can try to figure out what is wrong and fix it enough to get to a mechanic.

If you need to add coolant or water and the engine is still hot, stop. Turn off the engine and let the car cool down. If you add cold water to a hot engine you can crack the engine block and you will need a new engine. One common false notion is that if you keep the engine running and add cold water it will be okay, as the water will heat up before it reaches the engine. On the contrary, with the engine running the cold water will hit the engine block faster and you have a better guarantee of cracking the block!

Look under your hood and point out the radiator, the water pump, the hoses, and the fan. If the car is cool open the radiator cap, turn the engine on. Do you see the water flowing? That is the cooling system flowing.

Let's clearly define the component parts to the cooling system.

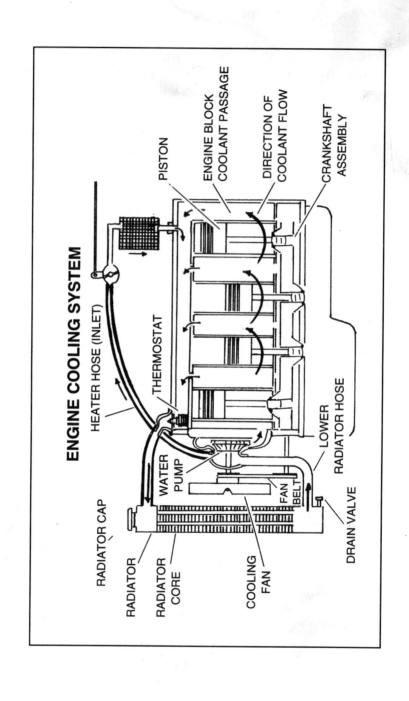

ENGINE COOLING SYSTEM

RADIATOR CAP

RADIATOR

RADIATOR CORE

COOLING FAN

DRAIN VALVE

HEATER HOSE (INLET)

THERMOSTAT

WATER PUMP

FAN BELT

LOWER RADIATOR HOSE

PISTON

ENGINE BLOCK COOLANT PASSAGE

DIRECTION OF COOLANT FLOW

CRANKSHAFT ASSEMBLY

1. The radiator stores the coolant which is cooled down by being open to the cool air from the road as the car moves forward. It has a pressurized cap to keep the water contained. When the hot coolant comes from the engine into the radiator, the radiator gets hot and this causes a lot of pressure, enough to sometimes blow a hole in the radiator, springing a leak.

Never attempt to open the radiator cap when the engine or radiator are hot as you can get severely burned.

2. The radiator fan fans the radiator fluid to cool it off.

3. The radiator hoses carry the fluid to and from the engine.

4. The engine is encased in a water jacket that circulates the coolant around the engine to keep it cooled off.

5. The water pump moves the coolant from the engine toward the thermostat.

6. The thermostat monitors the temperature of the fluid surrounding the engine and when the temperature gets to about

180 degrees it opens a valve letting the hot fluid flow back into the radiator.

7. This then pushes the cooler fluids out of the radiator and through the hose into the water jacket around the engine.

Sometimes mechanics have been known to take the thermostat out completely when it is broken, presumably on the basis that the water/coolant will now flow freely and keep cooled by the radiator. This is false: if there is no thermostat this can cause overheating because the fluid goes through the radiator so fast it does not have time to cool down inside the radiator. Also without a thermostat the choke can keep turning on and off when it is not needed, and cause poor gas mileage.(The choke is a valve that regulates the air flow to the combustion chamber. If the choke goes on unnecessarily it will cut off the air, and the fuel in the cylinders burns inefficiently, requiring more gas to be burnt. And there goes your gas mileage).

Radiators don't rust, but they will corrode slowly. Change the coolant once a year to flush the system out.

The cooling system also contributes to the passenger compartment by providing the heat source for your heater. As the hot coolant flows back to the radiator it passes through the heater. The heater fan uses this heat to blow hot air into the passenger compartment.

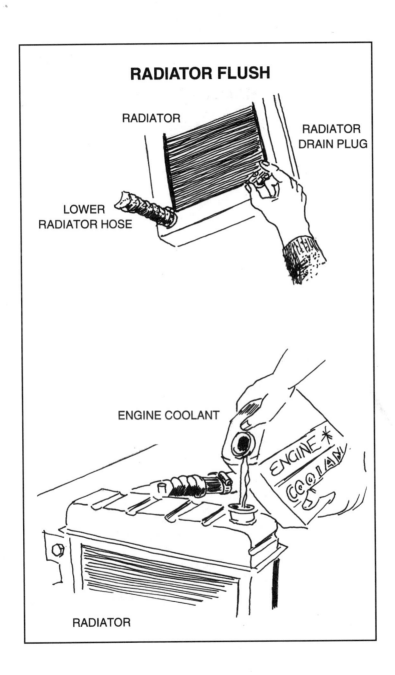

RADIATOR FLUSH

RADIATOR

RADIATOR DRAIN PLUG

LOWER RADIATOR HOSE

ENGINE COOLANT

ENGINE COOLANT

RADIATOR

RADIATOR CAP

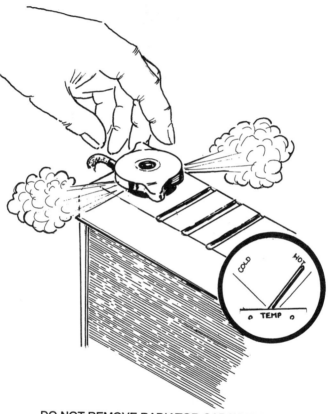

DO NOT REMOVE RADIATOR CAP WHEN THE
ENGINE IS AT NORMAL OR OVERHEATED
TEMPERATURE - SEVERE SCALDING MAY OCCUR

Chapter 8. The Lubrication System

The lubrication system is equal in importance to the cooling system. The oil in your engine prevents the hot metal parts from melting or welding together from the heat, friction, and pressure. Without oil your car engine will seize—stop moving. The metal parts, having no lubrication left, will just weld together and that is the end of your engine.

So if rule #1 is never let your car run out of or run low on coolant, rule # 2 is never let your car run out of or run low on oil.

Bearings

All moving parts in your car have bearings. These are either in the form of ball bearings or plate type bearings. These bearings surround the moving parts of the car creating a small space or a friction buffer that gives enough room for the oil to lubricate the moving parts. This way you never have metal directly touching metal. Oil itself is basically a type of ball bearing. If you were to look at oil under a microscope it would reveal millions of tiny balls. So you can think of oil as a liquid ball bearing that keeps the moving engine parts moving smoothly.

A certain pressure of oil is going through the engine all the time and the oil passages can get blocked up. Carbon build up can get in the oil causing the oil to get "dirty", and the oil will then lose its lubricating quality to a degree and may stick to the metal parts in the engine instead of lubricating them. That is why it is important to get the proper oil changes for your car at regular intervals.

The engine is the heart of the car. If the oil gets dirty and carbon is allowed to build up the oil will cease to flow. The phenomena will be similar to a blocked artery, and unless you give it a blood transfusion of fresh oil the condition is likely to become terminal! Forget about oil additives. You have to keep the oil clean and free of carbon. Change it regularly and your bearings and other moving engine parts will be happy.

CHAPTER 9. THE TRANSMISSION/THE GEARBOX

The transmission, of course, connects to the engine in the exact way that the engine connects to the transmission:

- The piston connects to the rod.

- The rod is connected to the crankshaft.

- The crank is connected to a fly wheel that is connected to a clutch.

- The clutch is connected to the gear-box or transmission.

- The gear-box connects via the driveshaft to the differential. The differential is just another type of gear that transfers the right amount of power to each of the wheels.

- The differential controls the axles. The axles are the connectors between the wheels.

The piston moves the rod, which moves the crankshaft, which moves the flywheel, which (via the clutch and gear-box) moves the driveshaft, which moves the differential, which moves the axles. The axles turn the wheels. The car moves. **Voila!**

Stop by your mechanic again. If he has a car up in the air on a rack ask him to point out the transmission system to you.

The Clutch

The clutch is a disc. When the pad is released, by the driver releasing the clutch, it lets the engine connect with the transmission. (This occurs automatically in an automatic transmission).

Clutch in = no power transferred

The clutch sits on a spring. As soon as the spring is released, by the driver letting out the clutch pedal, the clutch assembly connects to the fly wheel and thus the engine. When the clutch pedal is pushed in no power can be transferred from the engine to the transmission. If the car is already moving the car will continue to coast with the clutch pushed in, but there is no new transfer of power from the engine, and the driver has less control of the car.

Clutch out = power transferred

When the clutch is engaged (meaning the clutch has been let out by the driver) the engine power is transferred to the transmission. Now the car can move forward, or backwards.

THE CLUTCH

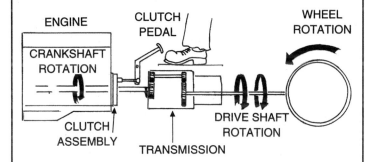

ENGINE   CLUTCH PEDAL   WHEEL ROTATION

CRANKSHAFT ROTATION

CLUTCH ASSEMBLY

TRANSMISSION

DRIVE SHAFT ROTATION

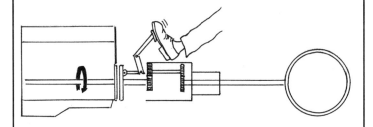

ON A STANDARD TRANSMISSION CAR
WHEN YOU PRESS THE CLUTCH PEDAL DOWN,
IT TAKES THE CAR OUT OF GEAR.

The pad (the clutch) gets worn after a period of time. This pad must be in good condition to properly grip the gears of the gear-box. The length of time the clutch will last without having to be replaced depends on how you use it. Never "ride" the clutch. Riding the clutch means to keep your foot on the clutch while the transmission is in gear. When you shift gears on a manual transmission always let your foot off the clutch as quickly as possible. You may have to "ride" it in first gear to some degree but try not to do so any more than is absolutely necessary to prevent the car from stalling. Get off the clutch as fast as possible when changing up and down all other gears. If you keep your foot on the clutch even lightly there will be friction between the clutch plate and the shaft that goes to the gear-box and the clutch pad will wear out.

The Gear-box and the Gears

The engine generates power or potential motion. The gear-box is the secret weapon that multiplies that power into high speed driving. Let us look for a moment at how gears work together and all will become crystal clear. Gears are made to "mesh". This means the teeth of one gear fit into the teeth on another gear.

Fewer teeth = turns faster

More teeth = turns slower

As you can see from the illustration, if a gear with 20 teeth is meshed with a gear with 10 teeth, the smaller gear will make twice as many revolutions as the larger gear. By the time the gear with ten teeth has revolved two times the big gear will only have revolved once. The number of teeth in one gear compared to the number of teeth in the gear it is meshing with determines how much faster the smaller gear will revolve than the larger one, or how much slower the larger gear will turn than the smaller one.

For example:

- A gear with 6 teeth will revolve 3 times as fast as a gear with 18 teeth with which it is meshed.

- A gear with 16 teeth will turn four times as slow as a gear with 4 teeth with which it is meshed.

As we have seen there is a crankshaft on the engine that revolves thousands of times per minute. If the crankshaft turns at certain RPMs and connects to a smaller gear then the drive train, and thus the wheels, will turn much faster than they would if connected to a larger gear at the same RPMs.

To conjure up some figures, for example only: let us say the first gear in a car has **30 teeth** and when the engine is turning at **3,000 RPMs** the car travels at **10 miles per hour.** Now let's say you shift to a second gear with half as many teeth (**15 teeth**) as the first gear. You can expect that at the same engine RPMs (**3,000 RPMs**) the car would move about twice as fast (**20 miles per hour**). In other words: half the teeth—same RPMs—twice the speed. Remember the revolutions per minute of the crankshaft. It is the crankshaft to which the different gears are connected. As the crank revolves it causes the connected gear to turn also. (Please! These are imaginary figures for the sake of understanding the principle, not the actual size of gears or speeds obtained).

Let's see how this works in practice:

In order to get a motionless car into motion a lot of power is required. The gearbox contains a main gear that connects to the crankshaft, receiving the power from the engine. The various gears (first, second, third, and so on) mesh to this main gear, picking up the power and converting it to motion. First gear is large enough to give the initial thrust required. Putting the car in gear makes the drive shaft of the transmission turn, which then makes the wheels move.

Torque: Since you have probably come across this term and most people have an awful time with it let's get it defined. It is actually a very simple concept. A corkscrew pushes forward with force in a twisting or turning fashion That is called torque. In a transmission the thrust of force from the engine is

GEARS, RPMs AND SPEED

 AT 3000 RPMs IN
1st Gear
SPEED IS
ABOUT 10 MPH

 AT 3000 RPMs IN
2nd Gear
SPEED IS
ABOUT 30MPH

 AT 3000 RPMs IN
3rd Gear
SPEED IS
ABOUT 45 MPH

 AT 3000 RPMs IN
4th Gear
SPEED IS
ABOUT 60 MPH

transferred by the gears to create a turning force that causes the drive train of the transmission to revolve. This power is carried forward to the wheels. The term used for this turning force is torque.

An automobile engine has a limit of the maximum RPMs at which it can comfortably revolve. As the car picks up speed the engine RPMs increase. Using the large first gear the engine would reach its RPM limit with the car only moving at about 10 or 15 miles per hour.

This is where second gear comes in. The car is shifted from first gear to second gear. Second gear has fewer teeth. So it turns faster and will reach higher speeds of travel than first gear did at the same RPMs of the engine. The car gathers more speed. Soon the engine again starts to turn at too high a level of RPMs.

The same trick is used. The second gear is disengaged and taken out of the loop. The driver pushes in the clutch, moves the gear stick out of second gear and pops it into third gear. (In an automatic transmission these gears shift automatically). Third gear is even smaller, less teeth. This allows the drive train and wheels to again move faster and the car to go faster while the engine can stay in a comfortable range of RPMs.

The same principle is applied to fourth and fifth or higher gears (in some sports cars and trucks).

To slow the car down (in combination with correct use of the brakes) you reverse the process and take the smaller gears out and put larger ones

PRINCIPLES OF GEAR ROTATION

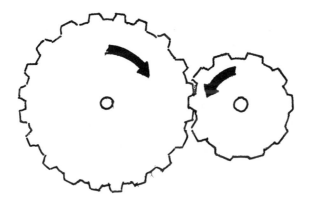

TEETH FROM ONE GEAR MESH WITH THOSE
OF ANOTHER

THE RATE OF ROTATION IS DETERMINED BY
THE NUMBER OF TEETH ON ONE GEAR
COMPARED TO THE OTHER

in place. The larger gears have more teeth and thus revolve more slowly. Even though you are "down shifting" the engine will compensate for the slower gear by working harder momentarily. So when you shift the gears down you can hear the RPMs of the engine increase while the car slows down. The engine is now working harder, but with the larger, slower gear connected, the drive train and thus the wheels move slower. (Reverse gear of course is another gear that just turns in the opposite direction. So the drive train pushes in the opposite direction and the wheels move backwards).

The gear system is a way of multiplying the power of the engine to turn the wheels faster (when shifting up) while the engine RPMs stay in a comfortable range, or a way of cutting the power to turn the wheels slower (when shifting down).

Let's recap this:

1. The engine crankshaft turns at a certain speed depending on how much gas is pushed into the engine and burned, as controlled by the accelerator.

2. To start the car moving a large, but slow, powerful gear takes the power from the crankshaft and sends it via the transmission to the wheels. This is first gear.

3. The engine RPMs increase to a maximum comfortable level, but the car is not going fast enough.

4. The driver switches to the second gear which is smaller, less teeth. It turns faster allowing the drive train and wheels to turn faster while the engine stays in the comfort zone of RPMs.

5. The RPMs increase and the car goes faster, but again the engine starts to over-work. The procedure is repeated of moving a smaller, faster gear into place which gets more speed to the wheels with less effort on the part of the engine.

Neat trick, eh!?

The key points to remember are:

1. Larger (lower) gears are more powerful and have greater thrust or torque; but they move slower and have a limit to how fast they can move the car forward without overworking the engine.

2. Smaller (higher) gears are less powerful and create less torque; but having fewer teeth, they move faster and can increase the speed of travel without making the engine work as hard.

An Automatic Transmission

An automatic transmission consists of a set of gears, clutches, and valves housed together in one sealed unit. Usually there are three gears, sometimes a fourth for "over-drive." These are set up so that the gears will shift up or down on a pre-set basis.

There are three factors that determine when the automatic transmission will shift up or down.

1. Road speed. A special type of gear called a "governor" monitors the road speed of the car. When this governor registers a pre-set speed the transmission will shift up to the next gear.

2. When the driver brakes or slows down and the road speed drops below a pre-set level the car will shift back down to a lower gear.

3. If the driver kicks down hard on the accelerator the automatic transmission is set up to shift down to a lower gear in order to give a sudden boost of power for faster acceleration. Then quickly it will shift into the next gear up. You sometimes get a slight "jump" effect as the transmission jerks into the next gear.

Pressure from the transmission fluid operating certain valves determines when the shifts occur, this pressure changing based on the road speed and the kick down of the accelerator as explained above. The chief enemy of the automatic transmission is loss of the transmission fluid, which in turn results in a build up of heat. This causes friction and wear, with tiny particles getting ground into the transmission or the fluid. This is why it is so vital to check the fluid and keep it topped up, and to get the fluid changed annually, so as to keep your automatic transmission in good shape. Synthetic transmission fluids are more resistive to heat. Refer to your manual for the specific fluid recommended for your car.

Towing automatics

Some very important warnings that can save you a lot of money if your automatic car ever has to get towed are:

- If your car is front wheel drive attach the tow truck only at the front and tow the car only from the front.

- If your car is rear wheel drive tow it only from the rear, backwards.

Here's the reason why:

If you tow a front wheel automatic backwards or a rear wheel drive from the front you are actually causing the transmission to turn as though the car is on, but no transmission fluid is circulating. Doing this for several miles can ruin the transmission. Tow truck drivers do not necessarily know this!

Transferring the Power to the Wheels

We have seen how the drive-train takes the power generated by the engine (via the rod, via the crankshaft, via the clutch) to the gearbox, which magnifies the power received using the gears. This power is now sent to the axles and the wheels to drive the car forwards or backwards.

Types of drive

Cars are either front-wheel drive, rear-wheel drive, or four-wheel drive. Front-wheel drive means the power that moves the car forward is directed by the transmission to the front wheels. Rear-wheel drive means the power is directed to the rear wheels. Four-wheel drive means all four wheels are provided with driving power by the transmission.

Differential

In a front-wheel drive car there is a differential on the front axle. A differential is a type of gear that simply distributes the power received by the axle to each of the wheels. It senses how much power to give to each of the wheels. The driving wheels in a car (be it front-wheel, rear-wheel, or four-wheel drive) can turn at different speeds. One of the wheels will spin faster when it needs more power to grip the road, for example when turning or driving over rough ground. The differential essentially "senses the difference" between the speed of spin of the two wheels and will direct more power to the wheel that is spinning faster, as this is the one that is needing more power in that situation.

In a rear-wheel drive the differential is on the rear axle, and it works the same way. A four-wheel drive has both a front-wheel and a back-wheel differential and so can direct power to both the front and the rear wheels.

A front wheel drive in most cases handles better than a rear-wheel drive. It will not spin out as easily and it will allow you to accelerate out of a corner, whereas a rear-wheel drive car will tend to spin out. Certain luxury cars that have a tradition of rear-wheel drive have kept to this tradition. Sophisticated suspension is often used to compensate. It may not entirely overcome the problem especially in adverse weather.

Chapter 10. The Exhaust System

Once the fuel and air mixture is ignited and burned in the engine cylinders, there is a residue left of poison gases such as carbon monoxide (a key ingredient of smog). Each cylinder has an exhaust valve for expelling this residue.

A pipe is connected to each of the exhaust valves and these four pipes combine into one pipe. This is known as the exhaust manifold. ("Mani" = many and "fold" = parts, thus manifold literally means "many parts.")

Catalytic converter

The residue is channeled from here to a piece of machinery known as the catalytic converter. ("Catalytic" means acts as a catalyst. A catalyst is something that speeds up a chemical reaction. In this case the chemical reaction is the converting of the poisonous gases in the exhaust to reduce the level of poisons and harmful chemicals released into the air). The catalytic converter consists of a honeycomb of holes made of platinum and ceramic. When the exhaust hits the catalytic converter some of the poisons are burned off.

Muffler and tailpipe

What is left is passed through the muffler to the tail-pipe and is expelled out the back of the vehicle. By no stretch of the imagination does the catalytic converter entirely take care of the environmental destruction caused by the poisons that are emitted, but it would be worse yet without these converters. When a smog test is done it determines if the catalytic converter is performing to the required standard as set by state and federal regulations. The muffler is simply a box with packing inside that deadens noise. It's just a sort of "silencer" for your car.

EXHAUST SYSTEM

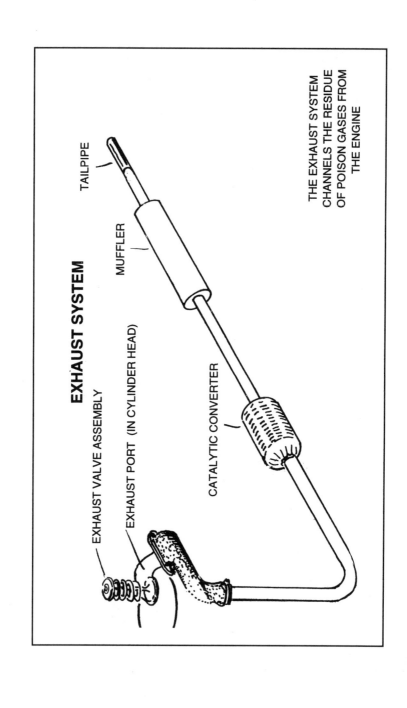

TAILPIPE

MUFFLER

EXHAUST VALVE ASSEMBLY

EXHAUST PORT (IN CYLINDER HEAD)

CATALYTIC CONVERTER

THE EXHAUST SYSTEM CHANNELS THE RESIDUE OF POISON GASES FROM THE ENGINE

CHAPTER 11. THE STEERING SYSTEM

Once the power reaches the wheels of your car you need to have precise control over where exactly your car is moving. The steering wheel attaches to a steering column. The steering column attaches to the steering box. There are a number of different types of steering mechanisms. They operate slightly differently but all are designed to allow the driver to control the direction of the car as he turns the steering wheel. Here is how one of the most popular types of steering systems (rack and pinion) operates. (We recommend you diagram this out for easier reading).

1. At the end of the steering column is a gear. This gear is called a "pinion".

2. The pinion teeth are meshed into a long shaft with continuous teeth. This is called a "rack".

3. When the steering wheel is turned by the driver the teeth of the pinion gear move along the teeth of the rack and push the rack right or left. If the steering wheel is turned right the pinion will push the rack to the left, in the opposite direction. If the steering wheel is turned to the left the rack will move to the right.

STEERING SYSTEM

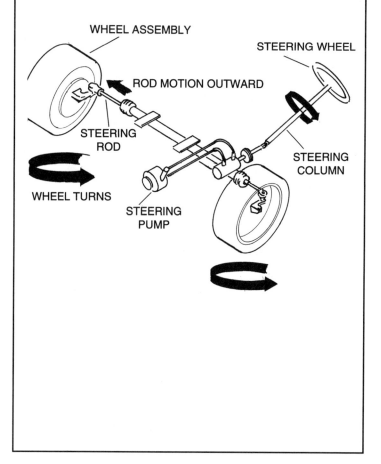

WHEEL ASSEMBLY

STEERING WHEEL

ROD MOTION OUTWARD

STEERING ROD

STEERING COLUMN

WHEEL TURNS

STEERING PUMP

4. The rack now pushes certain rods and bars that are connected to the rear portion of the driving wheels (the wheels on the ground that drive the car). These rods and bars push the rear of the driving wheel out. This of course makes the front of the wheel turn inwards. So if the rack moves left the rear of the driving wheel moves left but the front of this wheel moves right. Or if the rack moves right the rear of the driving wheel moves right but the front of the driving wheel moves to the left.

5. So if the steering wheel is turned to the left, the pinion moves the rack to the right, the rack pushes the rear part of the driving wheel to the right and so the front of this wheel (which sets the direction) goes to the left and the car moves to the left.

Power steering simply releases a fluid along the rack when the rack moves and the pressure of the fluid adds to the force with which the driver turns the wheel, making the wheel turn with less effort.

Alignment

Safe steering of the car depends on a correctly functioning steering column and a correct alignment of the front end of the automobile. Alignment means that the various bars used to steer with are straight, are of the correct length, are at the right angle, and so on. Alignment can be thrown off by hitting the curb or a pothole or other impact. When the alignment has gone out it is important that you discover WHY before simply getting an alignment done, as other damage may need repair. It is also vital to ensure that your wheels are properly balanced and that the tires are in proper working condition. Wheel balancing ensures the wheels turn in a true circle.

Chapter 12. The Braking System

Brakes are really just clamps. The wheels of the car are moving at high speed driving the car forward. The wheels are connected to the axles which revolve, turning the wheels. The brake disc or drum (these are just types of clamps) attaches to the axle. When you apply the brakes by stepping on the brake pedal you are applying a clamp to the disc or drum that, in effect, is holding the axle to keep it from turning. This of course slows down the rate at which the wheels are turning, eventually bringing them to a halt.

The brake pedal is connected by a cable to a valve that sits inside what is known as the master brake cylinder. The master cylinder contains fluid (brake fluid). When you press on the brake pedal this fluid gets compressed which makes the fluid denser or harder. The pressure of this fluid drives the braking system.

Disc brakes

Disc brakes are used on most cars now as they are more efficient and less subject to wear. The fluid moves from the master cylinder through the brake line pushing against a valve at each brake called a caliper. The calipers push the brake pads onto a rotor, which is a big disc. This causes friction as the pads grab the disc and the friction causes the car to stop.

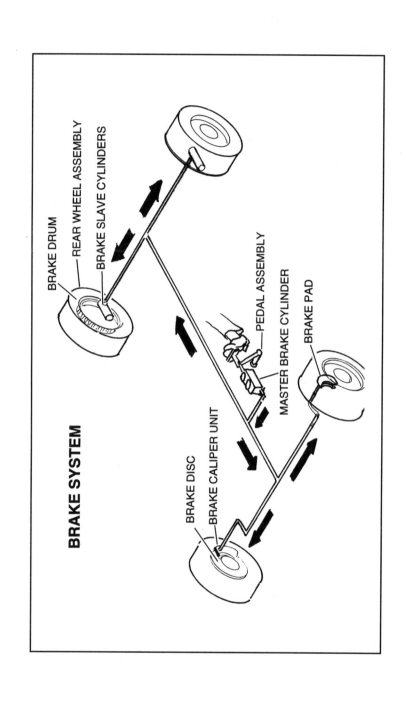

BRAKE SYSTEM

BRAKE DRUM

REAR WHEEL ASSEMBLY

BRAKE SLAVE CYLINDERS

PEDAL ASSEMBLY

MASTER BRAKE CYLINDER

BRAKE PAD

BRAKE DISC

BRAKE CALIPER UNIT

DRUM BRAKES

BRAKE DRUM

MASTER CYLINDER
ASSEMBLY

BRAKE SLAVE
CYLINDER

BRAKE LINE

PUSH ROD

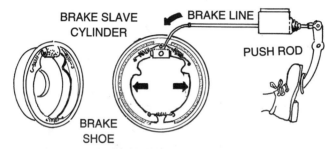

BRAKE
SHOE

DISC BRAKES

BRAKE CALIPER
ASSEMBLY

ROTOR (DISC)

BRAKE
LINE

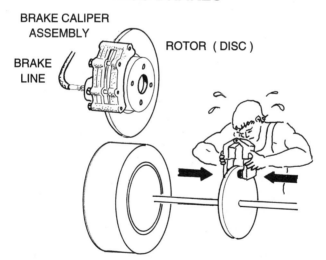

THE CALIPERS SQUEEZE THE BRAKE PADS AGAINST
THE ROTOR AND STOP THE ROTOR FROM TURNING.

Drum brakes

With drum brakes pistons tighten up against the caliper which pushes the brake pads into the brake "shoes". These press against rotating drums on the wheels expanding the drum and the friction stops the wheels. Drum brakes wear out a lot faster than discs.

ABS

You may see the term ABS. This stands for "anti-lock braking system." It is computer operated. It is a method of applying the brakes in a very fast, controlled pumping action—off and on every fraction of a second—so that even under severe emergency no matter how hard the brakes are depressed they cannot lock up.

Front and back brakes

There is only one master cylinder to the braking system, but there are two brake lines coming from it, one for the front brakes and one for the rear brakes. The front brakes are more important than the back brakes and more braking power is given to them. The ratio of braking power is approximately 60% directed to the front brakes and about 40% to the back brakes. If the back brakes have more power than the front brakes this will cause the car to go into a skid. So make sure that the brakes are working properly and the correct ratio of power exists between the front and back brakes.

Chapter 13. The Suspension System

The suspension system of the car has three functions:

1. To allow the driver to have smooth control of the car,

2. To increase the comfort of the ride, and

3. To protect the mechanical parts of the car from the shocks of the road.

The suspension system in older cars used to just consist of metal springs (rather like very strong bed springs). Later shock absorbers ("shocks" were developed consisting of a valve that contains oil or gas. As the car hits a bump or hole the springs absorb the shock of the motion. The "shocks" then actually absorb the motion of the springs, shortening the duration of the bouncing motion of the springs. The shock valves move down fast when a rough part of the road is encountered. The oil or gas then absorbs the shock and releases the valve slowly back to its normal position. This gives the passengers the sensation of a smooth ride. Essentially you are riding on a cushion of oil or gas. If you have ever dived into a swimming pool you know that the water breaks your fall, it absorbs the force with which you enter the water. The fluids or gases in the "shocks" work the same way.

These days the suspension system is designed to give independent suspension to all four wheels, greatly enhancing the car's ability to absorb the various shocks encountered. The shock absorbers are also very important in protecting the mechanical parts of the car from shock. Poor "shocks" are dangerous. If the "shocks" are gone you will have reduced control over the steering of the car especially at high speeds.

Test the "shocks" on your car. Push down hard on one side of the front of your car, over one of the wheels. Push up and down to get the car to bounce. Let go. Does the car bounce once and stop? It should. Repeat this with each corner of the car to test each shock. Does it bounce up and down several times? You need to get your "shocks" checked.

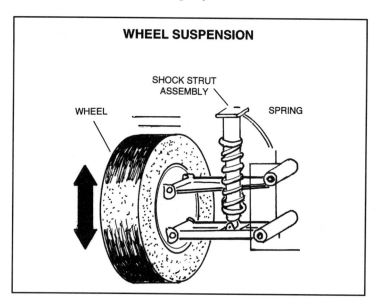

WHEEL SUSPENSION

SHOCK STRUT
ASSEMBLY

WHEEL   SPRING

CHAPTER 14. THE CAR BODY

Unibody

Many new cars these days are "uni-frame", built as a one piece unit and so they have no chassis in the old sense. Older cars are built on a chassis.

Chassis

The chassis is usually a ladder-like construction of steel, usually the strongest part of the car. It is like the foundation of a house. In a house, everything rests on the foundation.

Frame

The engine, the transmission, the various systems we have discussed, the exterior and the interior of the car are all bolted onto the chassis or onto parts that are in turn bolted onto the chassis. In uni-frame construction they are bolted directly onto the frame. The thing to know about the chassis is the importance of checking it if you are buying a used car. If a car has been in an accident the chassis or frame can get bent or cracked. This is very dangerous to drive. A car with a bent frame will not respond properly when steering and braking.

THE FRAME

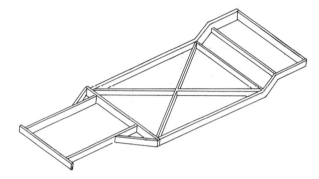

SIMPLE FRAME STRUCTURE (CHASSIS)

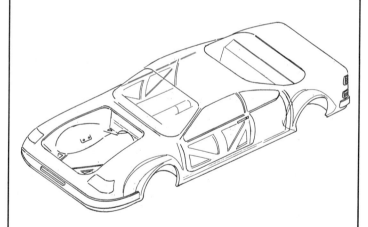

TYPICAL UNIBODY CONSTRUCTION

Exterior

The exterior of the car can be constructed of various materials, from heavy steel to light metal (known as tin cans) or even fiberglass. The heavier the material used, the stronger and safer in the event of a collision. On the other hand greater weight means more gas is consumed and the car is more expensive to run. Lighter materials have now been developed with more strength, but you will notice that the more expensive luxury cars are still constructed with heavy steel frames. An additional frame is often built these days around the passenger compartment and on some cars the outer frame is designed to deliberately collapse, thus absorbing some of the impact in the event of a collision. Of course the now collapsed car is not much use!

Decide for yourself what you want as far as safety and economy and choose your frame accordingly.

CHAPTER 15. THE INTERIOR

The interior of your car consists of:

1. **The seats** and other interior comforts. The seats have controls to adjust their position, height, and slant. Most cars have air conditioning, heaters, a radio, a cigarette lighter (which can also be used for accessories such as a cellular phone). Air conditioning works on the same principle as a small refrigerator, creating cold air that is blown into the interior of the car through the vents. Most cars are equipped with seat belts and many now have air bags that will inflate automatically in the event of impact to protect the driver from hitting the windshield.

2. **The dashboard**, which is the command center, informs the driver what is going on by means of various dials, lights, and symbols.

3. **The knobs, pedals, and other controls** with which the driver controls the car. There are controls by the steering column or on the dashboard for side lights, head lights, high beam head lights, directional indicators, hazard indicators, a manual or automatic gear stick, the steering wheel, the horn, the heater, the air conditioner, and the radio amongst others. The accelerator pedal, the brake pedal, and the clutch pedal are all located by the driver's feet. In case a fuse blows it is good to know that a fuse box is under the dashboard on the driver's side.

There are three vital things to know about the interior of your car:

1. Get familiar with all the controls and dials in your car. Nose around and find them. Look in the manual and find out what they do. Check them out. Make sure they are working properly.

2. If a light comes on the dashboard you must STOP and find out what the problem is. Do not keep on driving even if you are in a hurry. These lights mean something is wrong and you need to find out what. It could be serious.

3. If one of the controls is not working you need to fix it at once as these enable the car to be safely driven.

The Dials

The dials show the temperature of the engine, how fast the car is going, the RPMs, the mileage the car has been driven, and often such features as oil pressure and fuel consumption.

The speedometer shows the speed you are moving in miles or kilometers per hour. It has a counter that keeps a running total of miles or kilometers that the car has been driven. It also usually has a counter that you can use to measure the length of a particular trip. It is illegal to tamper with the

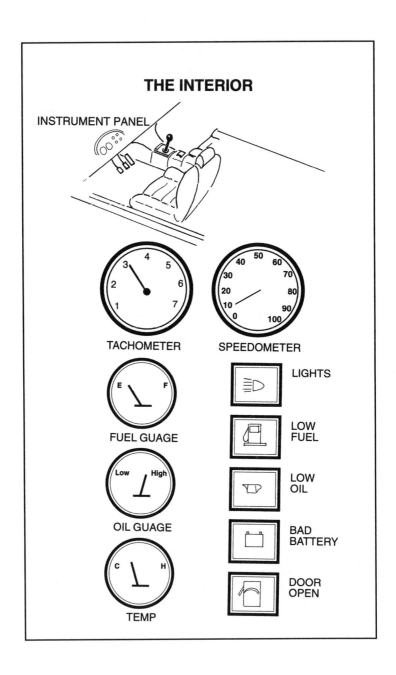

THE INTERIOR

INSTRUMENT PANEL

TACHOMETER

SPEEDOMETER

FUEL GUAGE

OIL GUAGE

TEMP

LIGHTS

LOW FUEL

LOW OIL

BAD BATTERY

DOOR OPEN

mileage counter, but sometimes people selling a car will move the mileage back to make the car appear more attractive. If you look carefully the numbers on the odometer should line up exactly in a straight line. If they do not the counter may have been tampered with. Does the mileage shown correspond to the age and conditions of the car?

The tachometer shows the RPMs of the engine to help you change gears at the right time.

The oil gauge shows the oil pressure. A normal oil pressure level is anywhere from about 45 pounds per square inch up to 75 pounds per square inch. If the oil pressure is showing below about 10 pounds per square inch then you must stop at once and locate the source of the low oil pressure. This could be as simple as checking the oil and filling it up. Normal and dangerous pressure levels vary from car to car and you should consult the manual for the levels for your car.

The temperature gauge shows how hot and cold the engine is. Do not let the engine overheat. If you see this gauge ranging higher than normal there is a problem and you must get it checked out fast.

The fuel gauge shows the fuel level in the tank and, sometimes in newer models, the fuel consumption occurring in miles per gallon.

The voltage meter shows the charge being sent back to the battery by the alternator and that the alternator is functioning properly. This gauge should not drop. There may also be a gauge showing if the battery is holding the charge it is receiving. This is different from the voltage meter.

There are a number of warning lights (sometimes called "idiot lights") on the dashboard that come on if the oil is low, the car is overheating, the voltage is bad, the gas is low and so forth. Once again do not ignore these lights if they come on. Find out why they are on and handle it now!

CHAPTER 16. THE BIG PICTURE

We have looked at the component systems of the automobile. Now let's review them again and how they fit together:

1. **The starter/ignition system** causes the car to start. It gets the engine to turn over; and the distributor to send electricity to the spark plugs.

2. **The fuel system** delivers the food to the lion (the engine). The fuel is pumped from the fuel tank via filters to the carburetor or fuel injection system and into the cylinders for combustion.

3. **The engine** takes the fuel and air in through the intake valves, explodes it, sends the power generated to the transmission so the car can move forward.

4. **The lubrication system** keeps the moving parts of the engine lubricated so they operate smoothly despite the heat and friction.

5. **The cooling system** keeps the engine cool so it doesn't overheat.

6. **The transmission or gear-box** takes the power from the engine and transmits it to the wheels for forward or backward drive.

7. **The exhaust system** gets rid of the poisonous waste from the combustion process.

8. **The steering system** enables the driver to direct where the car will go.

9. **The braking system** enables the driver to stop the car or slow it down as needed.

10. **The suspension system** protects car and riders from the roughness of the road.

11. **The electrical system** keeps the electrical power flowing where it is needed in the car.

12. **The chassis or frame** holds the whole machine together and provides the framework on which to build the interior of the car.

13. **The interior** gives the driver, who is the primary mind and brain of the vehicle, a place to sit and direct; and provides the driver with the information and controls he/she needs to run the vehicle.

Remember that these individual systems are carefully coordinated into a functioning whole. The timing of this coordination and the interaction between the systems is every bit as important as the individual systems themselves. In this way the energy is generated, magnified, converted, and passed on smoothly from one point to another. The car will then operate as an efficient, safe, and comfortable mode of transportation.

Hey, that's looking pretty simple now!

Self Test

Well, how would you like to do a self test on your knowledge to see how much you have retained? Don't worry. There are no teachers present and no-one is going to flunk you. Without looking at any of our illustrations draw a full page illustration of your own showing the major parts of an automobile and how they fit together.

Now compare that to our illustration. How did you do? If you missed anything major just go back and review the section that talks about that part, or review the whole book so far if you feel you need to or would like to.

Now answer these questions:

1. What is a solenoid?

2. How does a distributor work?

3. What part of the car re-charges the battery?

4. What passes through the carburetor?

5. What happens if the engine overheats?

6. What takes place inside the engine cylinders?

7. Why is it important to change the oil in your car on a regular basis?

8. What do RPMs measure?

9. What part allows the engine to connect to the transmission?

10. What does a differential do?

Look at the answers on the next page. If you missed on a few points no big deal, you may want to just go back and look those sections over again.

Write down a description of how "timing" works. Refer back to the section on timing and see how close you came.

O.K. By now you've got a pretty good understanding of how a car works. Are you ready to find out how to take care of one?

Test Answers

1. A solenoid is a switch that opens the flow of electricity to the starter motor.

2. A distributor takes the electricity from the battery and distributes it as a spark to each of the spark plugs.

3. The alternator re-charges the battery.

4. Fuel and air pass through the carburetor.

5. If the engine overheats the metal parts and seals will warp and melt. The head gasket will blow and the engine head will need to be resurfaced, or replaced if it cracks.

6. The pistons move up and down inside the cylinders. Valves let the fuel mixture in, the piston compresses it, and the spark from the spark plug ignites the fuel. The piston is forced down, transferring power to the crankshaft. The whole action takes place in four strokes of the piston inside the cylinder.

7. Carbon can get in the oil and it loses some of its lubricating quality and so can not protect the engine as well as it should from friction.

8. RPMs measure the number of revolutions per minute of the engine crankshaft.

9. The clutch allows the engine to connect to the transmission. When the clutch engages, it connects to the flywheel gear at the back of the engine, thus transferring the power from the crankshaft to the drive train.

10. **A differential** distributes the correct amount of power from the transmission to each of the wheels.

PART II - MAINTAINING YOUR CAR

CHAPTER 17. BASIC MAINTENANCE

Save money, Save time

From experience, keeping the proper basic maintenance on a car can prevent up to 80% or more of all mechanical breakdowns from occurring. This means that you can avoid up to 80% of your visits to your mechanic and the time this costs you, and you can save up to 80% of the money you spend on repairing your car. Reflect for a moment on how much time you have spent in the last five years taking your car to mechanics, waiting for the work to be completed, finding yourself stranded or delayed. Reflect on the amount of money you have spent in the last five years on mechanical repairs. Add it all up and you will probably agree that's a fair bit of wasted time and money that you could certainly have put to better use. Especially since you can avoid a large part of that TIME AND EXPENSE by simply following a few basic preventive routines.

Imagine if you never washed your body, never cleaned your teeth, never exercised, only ate junk food, never drank water, only slept one hour a night and so forth. Failure to take basic care of your body like that is likely to wind you up in the doctor's office or the hospital room sooner or later, probably sooner. Proper diet and exercise, fluids, hygiene and care, however will prevent a lot of potential physical maladies and is likely to give you a long, healthy, and trouble-free life. So it is with your automobile.

Having a familiarity with how your car should look, feel, and sound at its optimum is the way to greater control of your vehicle. Also, being able to quickly perceive what is wrong with it if it does go wrong. The best way to achieve this level of familiarity is to observe your car, feel your car, listen to your car, and take care of it by keeping up proper maintenance procedures.

NEW CARS

Breaking in your new car

The parts of a car consist of moving metal parts and so friction occurs as a matter of course. Breaking in a new car means that you handle it in such a manner that the moving parts are given the opportunity to gently and gradually work together, with the proper lubrication. Too much friction, heat, and pressure occurring too quickly before the car is acclimatized will cause damage from the start. An analogy would be going to an advanced aerobics class when you never exercise, or trying to run a world record marathon when you have never run more than a mile at one time.

Here are some rules to follow in breaking in your new car:

1. Check all fluid levels when you first get your car to ensure they are all to the full level. This means check the oil, the radiator and the radiator overflow, the transmission fluid, and the brake fluid.

2. When starting the car give it a minute to warm up.

The first 500 miles:

3. Do not accelerate hard or push the revs (engine revolutions) for the first 500 miles. Let the car accelerate gradually and gently.

4. Do not drive the car over 55 miles per hour for the first 500 miles.

5. At 500 miles get the oil changed, get all fluids fully checked and changed as needed, get all lubrication points lubricated.

6. Listen closely to your car engine, and transmission. Get attuned to how the engine and transmission sounds. If you hear any change in these sounds get the vehicle checked out at once.

7. After treating the vehicle this way for the first 500 miles you should be able to have it running at peak performance.

Maintenance on your new car

Often people who purchase a new car have the idea "great, a new car, it'll run for years and I don't need to do anything." It is a myth to believe that you are impervious to breakdowns because the car is new. Indeed you may have seen more than one almost-new car sitting sadly by the side of the highway and thought to yourself "wow, that car looks like it's almost new." On a new car you must check for all fluid levels at least once a week: water, oil, transmission fluid, brake fluid. If you hear any strange noises or feel anything unusual about how the car is running then get these levels checked at once.

Older Cars

Once a car is a year or so old it is time to increase the amount of basic checking that you do. If you are buying a car that is other than new then, of course, it has had other owners. You do not know how they have taken care of it. Perhaps well, and perhaps not. Many people (present company excepted, no doubt)) apparently take pleasure in running their car into the ground, until they realize the consequences in repair bills. Often that is the point they decide to sell it off and let someone else have the headaches.

When buying a pre-owned car you should get it thoroughly checked out and overhauled as necessary by a competent mechanic, particularly any safety points as well as the basics.

Daily routine

You should make a daily routine of checking the basic maintenance points on the car. It is possible for a car that is not brand new to develop a fluid leak without notice and if you check the fluid levels daily you are almost certain to catch this before it becomes a problem. All it takes is one water leak that goes undetected to cause the car to overheat and blow a head gasket, costing hundreds of dollars or thousands on more expensive cars. It only takes one undetected oil leak for the engine to seize requiring a new engine. It only takes one undetected brake fluid leak to cause a brake failure; and we won't discuss the possible consequences of that.

So check the fluid levels daily, before you leave the house. Then you won't have to take the chance of having to check them at the side of the freeway with a hot engine, arriving to your destination late, hot, sweaty, and dirty. Not a pleasant experience.

Sometimes the various dip-sticks for checking the fluids are well hidden, so it is a good idea to label the main fluid sticks with what they are and label the fluid containers with what goes in them. You can even paint the tops of the dipsticks with a bright color so they can't hide.

* * *

It may sound like we are going overboard on maintenance activities, but it really takes very little

time, and if you make it part of your routine you
will enjoy a more trouble-free relationship with your
car.

Let's look at the key maintenance activities
in more detail.

Coolant

Check this weekly on new cars, daily on cars
more than a year or two old. Always check this when
the car is cold. Open the radiator cap. Does the fluid
come all the way to the top? If not, top it up with
coolant. Check the radiator overflow container. Top
that up also if needed. If you are having to frequently
add coolant then you have an underlying problem
in your cooling system and you need to get this
looked into thoroughly.

Oil

Check the oil weekly on new cars, daily on
older cars. Look at your owners manual to determine which grade of oil you should use. Check the
oil by taking out the oil dipstick. Wipe it clean. In-
sert it back in fully again. Pull it back out and observe the level of oil against the markings on the
dipstick. It will tell you if the oil level is full or if it
requires adding oil. If you are having to add oil frequently then you have an oil leak or the car is burning oil.

Change the oil completely and replace the oil filter every 3 months or 3000 miles WHICH-EVER COMES FIRST. We recommend this strongly, no matter what any manual or mechanic might suggest to the contrary. You will more than save in repair bills for any money you spend on regular oil changes at 3 months or 3,000 miles.

Transmission Fluid or Oil

Check the transmission fluid in automatics weekly. Check it with the engine running. In cars that are a few years old we suggest that you check it every time you fill up at the gas station. If you have had any history of transmission problems then check it daily. There is a dipstick to check the fluid level. Using a special funnel that fits right into the filler that the dipstick sits in, keep it topped up. Synthetic fluid is recommended. If any quantity of fluid is getting used up then get the transmission fully checked out. Change the fluid once a year. In a manual transmission the gear oil is sealed into the gear box and there is nothing to check. Get this gear oil replaced once a year by your mechanic.

Power Steering Fluid

If you have power steering then you need to check the power steering fluid regularly. It is usually in a similar type of container as transmission fluid. If this fluid is getting used up a lot, or you

LUBRICATION SYSTEM MAINTENANCE

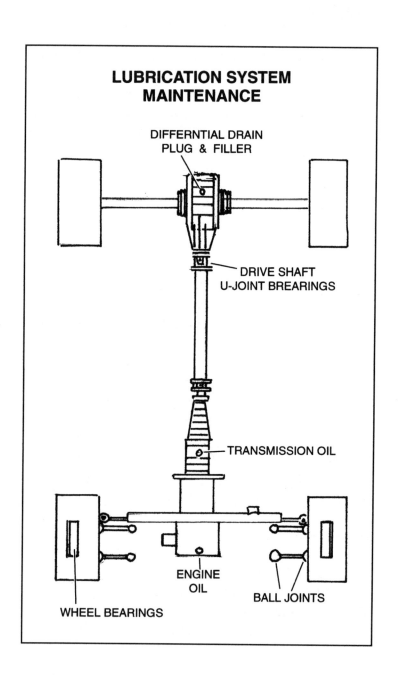

DIFFERNTIAL DRAIN PLUG & FILLER

DRIVE SHAFT U-JOINT BREARINGS

TRANSMISSION OIL

ENGINE OIL

WHEEL BEARINGS

BALL JOINTS

detect any problems with your steering column, such as a lack of smoothness or any noise, check it out at once.

Brake Fluid

Check this weekly in new cars, daily in older cars. There is another container that is similar to the transmission fluid canister. Make sure you have these clearly marked so they do not get confused. If you are having to add brake fluid you must get your brakes checked out and serviced to avoid the danger of accidents due to brake failure.

Tires

Check your tires every time you fill up at the gas station. Invest in a tire pressure gauge as most gas stations can supply you with air but few now have working pressure gauges. Look in the manual for the correct tire pressure for your car. Note that this pressure is usually based on using the recommended tire for that car. Of course that is the only type of tire you should use anyway. If you are going on a long journey the tire pressure should be a bit higher then normal. If you are carrying extra weight or hitching up a trailer then you must add additional pressure. Once you are back to normal weight don't forget to put the pressure back to normal.

Check your tires for wear. If the tires become worn on one side of the car more than the other you need to get an alignment. Tires also need to be correctly balanced. Tires can wear at one spot more than others or a wheel can get slightly chipped or scraped and cease to revolve in a true circle. This will cause the car to shake. Such a wheel needs to have small weights attached at the points it is out of true to allow it to revolve correctly again. This is called balancing. When you see a tire wearing down to the point that there are flat spots on the tire then it is time to change it. Never let a tire wear down to the metal underneath the rubber—the tire can explode as you are driving.

The only way in which you rotate radial tires (which means almost all tires today) is to move the back tires to the front wheels and the front tires to the back wheels. Never switch them from side to side. If your car is rear-wheel drive the back tires will wear down first. So when you see the back tires begin to wear a little rotate them with the front tires, as long as the front tires are in better condition. For front-wheel drive, when the front tires begins to wear a little, switch them with the back tires as long as the back tires are in better condition.

Battery

If your battery is not of the maintenance-free variety, you need to check the battery fluid level regularly and top up with distilled water only, as needed.

Windshield Fluid

Check this fluid regularly. Ensure your wipers are in good condition also, before winter hits.

Tune-ups

If you have a new car or if your car has been properly serviced according to the manual, then simply continue to service it according to those specifications. If your car is older and has not been serviced in this way then you need to get regular tune-up servicing. A good mechanic will do a thorough check, replacing only those items that require it.

Normally this will mean checking and probably replacing the air filter, the fuel filter, the distributor cap and rotor, the spark plugs and spark plug wires, the oxygen sensor on the exhaust manifold, adjusting the timing, changing the oil and oil filter, and lubrication of all the joints under the car.

Major tune-ups will involve the replacement of items such as timing belts, valve adjustments, and so forth. These can be checked each time you get a tune-up but timing belts should only have to be replaced approximately every 50 to 60,000 miles.

Exterior and Interior Maintenance

Your car will appreciate being regularly cleaned and cared for on the exterior and interior. Washing the car, waxing it at regular intervals, detailing it from time to time will maintain the value of your investment as well as increase your affinity for the vehicle. When cleaning the exterior of your car use cloths or sponges. Do not use brushes. Any plastic, leather, or surfaces getting hit directly with sunlight should be wiped down with special creams once a month. To keep the dash in good condition you can get a dash cover.

Maintaining the Safety Features of Your Car

Uppermost in the minds of most people in importance is whether your car is running and reliable. Equally as important, however, are the safety features of your car and ensuring that these are in proper working order. While most of these have been mentioned elsewhere in the book, let's review all of these features together. All are crucial to optimum safety. An unsafe car is a lethal weapon both to yourself, your passengers, and your fellow drivers on the road. Do not neglect to immediately fix any problem with the safety features mentioned here.

The tires on a car are made of rubber, usually placed around a steel belt. The rubber wears down with use. The tires can wear unevenly for various reasons and it is important to know the different factors that can cause poor wear so as to be able to get this fixed properly.

Tire wear - if tires are over-inflated the tires will wear in the center of the tread more than at the edges.

Under-inflation - with insufficient air pressure the tires will wear at the edges of the tread.

Other patterns of wear can be caused by problems with alignment, wheel balance, brakes, or by other problems. Your professional mechanic should diagnose the exact situations that need to be handled.

The brakes must be in good working order, both front and back. Bad brakes will affect not only your ability to stop in time but also your ability to steer and control the car when braking.

The steering system must be mechanically sound and responsive to the driver's commands. Steering can be adversely affected also by poor brakes, worn tires, or a faulty suspension system. Adequate control of steering depends on proper front end alignment and an absence of any such problems as bad wheel bearings, tires, or wheels out of balance.

The horn must be audible and has saved the day on many occasions when its failure could have resulted in a serious accident. On the other hand, many a disaster has resulted from a horn that did not work.

All of **the lights** should be checked regularly. This includes side lights, head lights, high beam headlights, indicator lights, hazard lights, and reversing lights. If a light bulb has blown these can be easily replaced with a screwdriver in just a few minutes. If a light fixture has been damaged by an accident you should fix this as a priority.

Lights are vital to visibility. So are properly working windshield wipers and blades, windshield fluid dispenser, a windshield that is free of cracks, mirrors that give you adequate rear view, and a properly working defrosting system. These points should all be checked regularly and any problems fixed well before rain comes.

Whether or not you agree philosophically with the compulsory wearing of seat belts, statistically they have been proven to save lives and lessen the severity of damage to persons in an accident.

The environment

Cars that use petroleum based fuels will never be good for the environment, but until we have a proven, better, and affordable alternative we still need to avoid all possible harm to the environment. (We won't discuss here the politics of whether certain vested interests would try to suppress a better solution). Here is how we can all contribute:

1. If your car is burning oil get it to a mechanic.

2. Keep your catalytic converter in proper working order and get the required smog checks.

3. If you see someone emitting a lot of exhaust then try to point out to them (while avoiding hostilities) that they are harming the environment and that this adversely affects themselves and their family, as well as the rest of us.

Maintenance Checklists

Daily (unless car is new)

      oil level is full

      coolant level is full

      coolant overflow is full

      horn is working

      all lights are working

      indicators are working

      windshield wipers and washers are working

      mirrors are clean

      window visibility is fine

      tires look and feel OK

      brakes feel OK

      steering feels OK

Weekly

      Brake fluid level is full

power steering fluid level is full

transmission fluid level is full

windshield fluid level is full

windshield wipers are OK

tire pressure is correct

tire condition OK (not worn)

no cracks in windshield/windows

seat belts are working, no damage

suspension checks out OK, all corners

Periodic maintenance:

Every 3 months or 3,000 miles whichever is sooner:

oil and filter changed

lubrication

check belts

check for any leaks, frayed wires, etc.

Every 6 months or 10,000 miles, whichever is sooner:

> tune-up service:

> replace spark plugs

> replace/clean air filter

> check timing

> check distributor/cap

> check fuel filter

Annually:

> replace brake fluid

> replace power steering fluid

> replace transmission fluid or oil

> flush radiator and replace coolant

Chapter 18. Basic Simple Repairs

This chapter covers basic simple repairs that can be done by just about anyone, covering in the process some basic tools and how to handle them. This is not intended by any means to be a comprehensive repair manual or to be a substitute for a good mechanic. They are mainly procedures that will help you out if you get stranded on the side of the road and will get you going again so you can get to an auto service station.

The key to handling the repairs in your car is to look at and become familiar with every part of that car. Then you can decide what you feel you can handle in an emergency. If you feel you could handle a certain repair the motto should be *"be prepared for it."*

A tool and emergency kit

The first thing you will need is a tool and emergency kit. If you don't have the repair manual for your car try to get it from the manufacturer. Then you should go to your local auto repair store. You will need a set of sockets, a set of wrenches and pliers. Get a set of screwdrivers and a vise-grip. Get good quality tools. Cheap ones will just fall apart. Foreign cars require metric tools. Look at all the nuts and bolts in the car and find out the different sizes of the bolts you can reach and get the tools to fit these nuts and bolts.

You will need flares and signs in case you break down, to warn other traffic. A flashlight is vital. Measure across the top of your hoses and get a length of flexi-hose that is the right diameter. There is also product called hose tape that will hold together a leaking hose until you can get it replaced. A tire gauge should be included. For an emergency only, there is a quick fix product that you can squirt into a leaking tire that will prevent you from being stranded. Find out where your jack is located and learn how to use it. Make sure it is not seized up; and that you have a lug wrench with which to take off the tires. Ensure the spare tire is in good condition. Find out where the jack points are on your car so that if you need to use it you can set up the jack so it won't fall on you. This data should be in the car manual or you can find out from your mechanic.

Do not carry spare gas with you. If the car gets hit and rear-ended the gas is likely to explode and if it is in the trunk it is in fact inside the car. This is quite dangerous. A spare quart or two of oil is O.K. If your car is burning a lot of oil, though, you need to get it fixed, for the car's sake and for the environment. It is O.K. to carry coolant with you (but don't have any opened coolant where children can get at it—it is poisonous).

How to correctly jump start your car

There is an exact way to correctly jump start a car. If it is done improperly you can burn out the

TOOL KIT

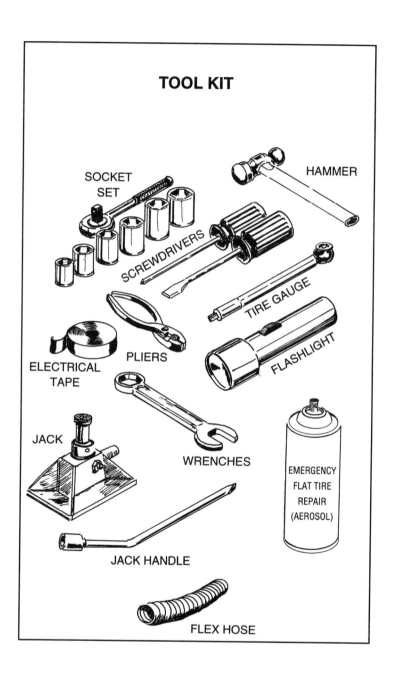

SOCKET SET

HAMMER

SCREWDRIVERS

TIRE GAUGE

PLIERS

FLASHLIGHT

ELECTRICAL TAPE

JACK

WRENCHES

EMERGENCY FLAT TIRE REPAIR (AEROSOL)

JACK HANDLE

FLEX HOSE

electrical system or blow up the battery. There are two terminals on a battery. The positive terminal and the negative terminal. When you jump start a car you are connecting up one battery, and transferring electrical power, to another battery. You must connect the positive terminal on the one battery to the positive terminal on the other; and the negative terminal on the one battery to the engine block on the other. If you connect up the positive to the negative or the negative to the positive you will blow things up.

You need to know which is negative and which is positive for both batteries and for the jumper cables. The jumper cables are usually marked red for positive and black for negative. Batteries are not usually color-coded but are usually marked with a plus sign for positive and a minus sign for negative. Make sure you have these all correctly located with certainty before attempting the jump start procedure:

1. Leave the ignition key turned off on the car with the dead battery.

2. Turn on the engine of the car with the good battery.

3. Connect the leads of the jumper cable to the good battery, positive to positive and negative to negative.

4. Now connect the positive terminal at the other end of the jumper cables to the positive terminal on the dead battery. Connect the negative terminal on the jumper cables to the engine block. Do not connect it to the negative terminal on the battery because it can damage electrical components that way.

5. Now let the good battery charge the dead one for several minutes, before you turn on the ignition. This gives a chance for the dead battery to get some juice in it and when you turn the car on there is less stress on the alternator.

6. Now turn on the ignition key to the car with the dead battery and start the car. It may take a couple of tries for enough juice to get through.

7. Take the jumper cables off the battery that had to be charged. Then off the battery that was used for charging.

8. Get your car to the auto-shop and get the battery, the alternator, and the entire electrical system checked out. If there is an alternator problem the battery will quickly go dead again. If there is a short in the electrical system it can ruin your battery, ruin your alternator, and start a fire.

How to clean off battery terminals

Battery terminals can develop corrosive buildup from acid. This can prevent the proper functioning of your battery. To clean them off you can simply use hot water. Using a wrench, take the cables off the terminals. Put a rag around one of the terminals while you clean the other because if you get water between the two terminals you will short out the battery. Wash off the worst of the corrosion and then clean the terminal with a stiff brush. Now put the rag around the terminal you have just cleaned and wash off the other one. Also clean the inside of the cables that connect to the battery terminals. The cables can get frayed as well, so inspect them and replace as needed. Ensure the cables are tightly connected. Loose cables won't conduct the flow of electricity properly. After tightening the cables, to help prevent a further build-up of corrosion on the terminals, you can pack the terminals with grease.

How to change a battery

Changing a battery applies the same principles as jump starting a battery. You have to make sure you know which electrode on the cable is positive and which is negative; and which electrode on the battery is positive and which is negative. Put a dab of red paint on the positive and a dab of black paint on the negative for each electrode.

Simply loosen the electrodes on the battery and slip them off. Make sure the cables are free of corrosive acid build up. You can wash them off with hot water if needed and then dry them. Remove the old battery. Put the new battery in its place. Ensure you put the positive cable onto the positive electrode of the new battery and the negative cable onto the negative electrode of the new battery. Tighten the cables and your new battery is ready to go!

How to change a flat tire

Before you can change a flat tire you must have:

a) A working jack that you know how to use, including where to place the jack so it is safe and stable. Check your manual for this information.

b) A spare tire which is kept in good and usable condition. Tires that have been discarded as unfit for the road are too often made into the spare tire.

You should practice changing a tire in your driveway or garage until you feel confident about it so you will have no trouble if you have to do it at the side of the road.

1. Try to park on a flat piece of road to change tires.

2. Before jacking up the car, loosen the lug nuts while the wheels are still on the ground. Don't take them off, just loosen them enough so that when the car is raised you can take the nuts off easily. The longer your lug wrench, the easier it will be to loosen the nuts.

3. Raise the car up on the jack, take off the nuts, and remove the wheel.

4. Put the spare wheel in its place. Put the lug nuts on by hand and tighten just a little.

5. Lower the jack and use the lug wrench to tighten the nuts all the way. When you tighten them go from one nut to the next, tightening each one a little bit, then repeat this procedure several times around until they are all fully tightened.

6. Don't forget to get a new spare, or a new tire for the one that had to be replaced so you can return the spare to the trunk.

How to change the oil

This is quite a simple procedure. It can be messy so ensure you have a large oil pan to catch all the oil you remove, plenty of rags to wipe up spills, and don't wear a suit or an evening dress! Do the oil change in a location where you are not going to create an upset if a little oil is spilled. You can get oil stain remover from an auto parts store, though, so don't worry too much.

You will need jack stands to hold your car up safely after you have jacked it up. The jack stands are additional to the jack used to raise the car and are more stable.

1. Jack up the car and place the jack stands at the correct jack points.

2. Remove the oil pan drain plug (usually the largest bolt in the middle of the pan) and drain the oil into an oil pan.

3. Put a new washer on and tighten the oil pan drain plug.

4. Locate the oil filter. Take it off and replace it with the new filter, but not too tightly. Hand tight plus a quarter of a turn with a wrench is about right.

5. Fill up with the correct grade oil. Usually you will need approximately 4 or 5 quarts, but check your manual.

6. Start the engine for twenty seconds only.

7. Check the oil level again, as the oil filter can absorb up to a quart of oil. Fill it up to the full level on the dipstick.

OIL CHANGE

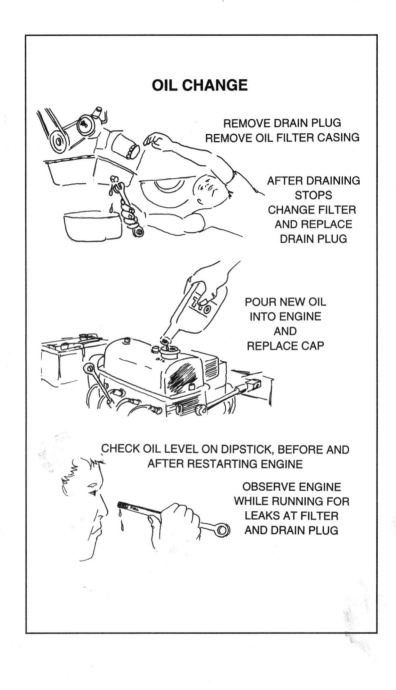

REMOVE DRAIN PLUG
REMOVE OIL FILTER CASING

AFTER DRAINING
STOPS
CHANGE FILTER
AND REPLACE
DRAIN PLUG

POUR NEW OIL
INTO ENGINE
AND
REPLACE CAP

CHECK OIL LEVEL ON DIPSTICK, BEFORE AND
AFTER RESTARTING ENGINE

OBSERVE ENGINE
WHILE RUNNING FOR
LEAKS AT FILTER
AND DRAIN PLUG

Always change the filter when you change the oil. Make sure that you have a container to put the old oil in and a safe way to dispose of it so children cannot get to it, and so it is safe for the environment.

How to flush out a radiator

1. Wait for the car to cool off before starting this procedure. If the radiator is fitted with a drain plug you can take out the plug and drain the coolant. If not, take the clamp off the lower radiator hose and drain from there. Drain the coolant into a container. It is poisonous and must be carefully disposed of. Do not put it down drains or toilets. Make sure children and animals are not around when doing this procedure, and that they cannot get at the coolant and drink it.

2. After draining the coolant, tighten the drain plug or re-clamp the radiator hose.

3. Fill the radiator with water and turn the engine on.

4. Run the engine until hot.

5. Let it cool off.

6. Drain it again and then tighten the drain plug or replace the hose.

7. Repeat this procedure until the water that comes out is clean.

8. Now put 100% coolant in the radiator and fill it up.

If you are in motion and the temperature gauge starts to rise slowly that most likely means your radiator is blocked up, and the radiator probably needs a "rod out." The radiator consists of a series of tubes and if 20% or so of these tubes get blocked up then the radiator will cease to function adequately. A radiator flush will sometimes work, if the blockage to the radiator is just loose debris, but it is more likely material that has caked onto the tubes of the radiator and hardened. A reverse radiator flush as described above will not handle this. It is rather like plaque on teeth—brushing will remove it to a certain point—then you need to get a professional cleaning at the dentist.

A "rod out" will push a rod down each of these tubes and force the blockage material out. This is usually done at a radiator shop and your mechanic should have a reputable, competent shop to which he sends out radiators for fixing.

CHAPTER 19. WHAT CAN GO WRONG

In this chapter we will take a look at just some of the major problems that can develop in the different parts of your car. We highly recommend that as we cover the different systems you refresh your memory and refer back to the corresponding section in Book 1.

* This section contains some information that is more technical and detailed, so ensure you have a firm grasp of the material covered so far in this book.

The starter and ignition systems

The starter and ignition systems exist to provide the initial crank to the engine, deliver the initial spark, and the initial burst of fuel. When you have problems getting a car started, the problem is:

a) electrical (covered in the next section)

b) the starter or its solenoid switch

c) you are not getting spark

d) you are not getting fuel

e) a combination of these factors

Starter problem

You can tell when the starter is about to go - it makes a rasping, crunching sound when you start the car. Let's explain what causes this. The starter motor pushes out a shaft with a gear attached to it. This gear connects with the flywheel and engages the engine. If the starter is worn this shaft and its gear will not move out fully. It is on a spring and it will move out slowly and catch the edge of the flywheel but it won't quite mesh. You try the starter a bit more and now it goes fully out and meshes. The rasping sound is similar to what you would hear if the car was already started and you turned the key again. Once you hear this crunching sound it is time to change the starter. The flywheel could have been damaged in the process so get this checked as well.

Fuel problem

To check to see if you have a fuel problem, take the air filter off and spray starter fluid into the carburetor (if your car has one). If it now starts right away, then you were not getting any fuel through the carburetor. This could be a carburetor fault, or a problem in the fuel line, the fuel pump, the fuel filter, or you simply ran out of gas. (Embarrassing, but it happens often enough!) If you have fuel injection, get it professionally checked by your mechanic.

No spark

If the car still does not start then you are not getting any spark. The problem here could be the coil, the distributor, or the electronic ignition if you have one of these. The coil is a booster that pushes electricity via the distributor to the spark plug. You have probably heard the term "rotor". This is a part that "rotates" in the distributor sending the spark in sequence to each of the spark plugs. This spark goes through tiny electrical contacts in the distributor cap. The rotor could need replacing or you may need a new distributor cap.

The problem could just be bad spark plugs that are fouled by oil or carbon, or just worn out.

The electrical system

Electrical system problems primarily consist of

a) a bad battery

b) a bad alternator

c) a bad wire

d) a blown fuse

Dead battery

We have already looked at what occurs when the battery goes dead; the continuous circuit of electrical flow from the "negative" terminal to the "positive" terminal in the battery, out to the car, and back through the alternator has been interrupted. It can break down within the battery, in the alternator, or due to a bad wire or other electrical malfunction somewhere in the car. The effect in any of these cases is that the chemical reaction ceases to occur in the battery. Sometimes you will be able to get the battery recharged if it goes dead. However for various reasons the battery may break down and lose its ability to re-charge and must be replaced. This can be checked on equipment that your mechanic will have.

Every piece of electrical equipment is receiving a flow of electrons through the wires that connect to it from the battery or the alternator. As we have seen with a battery there are two poles to electricity, the "positive" and the "negative". This is true for any piece of electrical equipment. For a piece of electrical equipment to work properly it must be connected to both the "positive" and the "negative" poles.

The "ground" or "earth"

The "negative" terminal on the battery is connected to the body of the car. This is called a "ground", because, since the body of the car sits on the ground, it is actually connecting the "negative" pole of the battery to the earth itself. Similarly every piece of electrical equipment has to be grounded properly, giving it its "negative" pole. All electrical parts of the car are also connected by wires to the body of the vehicle, thus completing the electrical circuit for that part. If a part is not grounded it will not operate.

A "short"

If a live wire connected to an electrical part gets exposed and touches a ground wire or touches any part of the body of the car (which will act as a ground), it creates what is called a "short." This means the full circuit of electricity is cut short and the parts connected to the short circuit will cease to function. If the live wire only occasionally touches the ground, as the car moves or shakes a certain way, the short will be intermittent (on and off). That part with the short will cause a drain of electrical power. The car can be turned off but the part will act as though it is turned on and the battery will get drained. Wires can get exposed due to friction, weather, and age. Shorts can be hard to find and electrical specialists are often called in to locate and repair the wiring.

Driving in the rain

Incidentally, if you are driving in rain and the car stalls, moisture has gotten into the distributor. This is just another type of short as the water conducts off all the electricity. The whole car just dies. If you spray WD40™ (from your auto parts store) into the distributor cap or wipe it out with a cloth it will work again. Similarly, steam cleaning an engine incorrectly can create a short, by getting electrical parts and wires wet. Go to a professional steam cleaner who has the equipment to ensure the car is properly dried out and no shorts exist before giving you back the car.

Fuses

Fuses exist to protect electrical circuits from overload. If there is an electrical malfunction too much electricity may get sent to an electrical part which could severely damage and ruin that part. To prevent this, if there is an overload the electrical flow is diverted through a fuse, which absorbs the overload but "blows out" in the process. Several different electrical parts may be connected to the same fuse. In this case, if one of the parts gets overloaded and "blows" a fuse, that entire electrical circuit and all the parts connected to it will cease to operate. It is easy to check for a blown fuse. Just go to the fuse box and open it up. It will list which fuses are for which parts. Take out the appropriate fuse and you can tell if it is blown. It will be cloudy and discolored. Just replace it with the same type of fuse (they are labeled) and it should fix the problem.

BLOWN FUSE

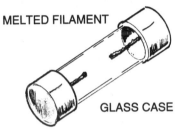

MELTED FILAMENT

GLASS CASE

CONTACT AREA

A SHORT

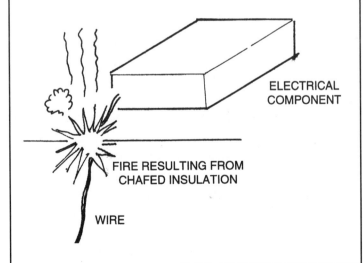

ELECTRICAL
COMPONENT

FIRE RESULTING FROM
CHAFED INSULATION

WIRE

Let's review:

1. If an electrical problem develops the battery will go dead and may or may not be re-chargeable. This can be checked by your mechanic.

2. Every piece of electrical equipment must be grounded or it will cease to work.

3. If a live wire gets exposed and touches metal or a ground it will short out. The car part involved will act as though it is using electricity even though it is not on. This can discharge the battery with the car turned off.

4. An overload of electricity hitting an electrical part will blow a fuse and this will need to be replaced.

What can go wrong with your alternator

The battery is in continuous use, putting out power while the car is on. The alternator returns more power to the battery than the battery puts out, keeping the battery charged. If you have a voltage dial on your dashboard this will show the amount of current being put out by the alternator. It should hold at about 13 and 1/2 volts. If the voltage meter is showing the correct voltage but your car will not start then the problem is with the battery. If the alternator is going bad then the battery will slowly

BAD ALTERNATOR

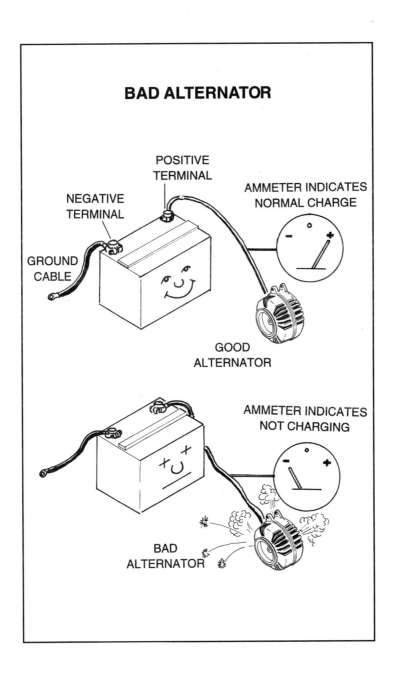

POSITIVE
TERMINAL

NEGATIVE
TERMINAL

GROUND
CABLE

AMMETER INDICATES
NORMAL CHARGE

GOOD
ALTERNATOR

AMMETER INDICATES
NOT CHARGING

BAD
ALTERNATOR

run down; the voltage gauge will start to drop. There is also a warning light indicator for the alternator on the instrument panel. If that light comes on while the car is still running then the alternator is not working. If the light comes on dimly then gets gradually brighter and brighter then your alternator is starting to go bad.

The alternator is driven by the alternator belt. If this belt breaks then—boom—there is a sudden loss of power as the alternator is no longer moving and will be unable to charge anything. If the battery goes totally dead and after you successfully jump start the car it still keeps working then the alternator must be good as it is keeping the battery recharged. However if the battery is bad and you keep driving on it then you are going to overwork the alternator and it will overheat and burn out. Even a brand new alternator will burn right out. Perhaps the mechanic fails to spot that the battery is no longer re-chargeable. He replaces the alternator which has been burned out trying to drive a dead battery, without replacing the battery. In a very short time you once again have a busted alternator.

Note: If the battery goes dead overnight then there is a short in the system or the interior light is jammed on (or you forgot to turn off the headlights!)

The fuel system

Fuel system problems are basically either too much fuel getting through, not enough fuel getting through, or using the wrong fuel.

If the carburetor is incorrectly adjusted the fuel/air mixture can give:

a) too much fuel/too little air; or

b) too little fuel in ratio to air (too lean).

If the air filter is blocked up too little air gets through compared to fuel and this will give too rich a mixture. Then the engine runs sluggish, burning too much fuel.

• If too much fuel gets into and sits in the carburetor the car can stall from lack of oxygen (called flooding).

• If too much air is getting in, in ratio to fuel, the oxygen will not get burned and will tend to oxidize the metal in the engine, and the valves can get burnt out.

• If too little fuel is getting through the car will tend to have poor power, cough, sputter, and die through lack of fuel. Fuel is energy is power. The fuel system can get blocked at any point either in the fuel lines, the fuel filters, the fuel pump, the carburetor, or fuel injection system.

Carburetor

If a carburetor problem develops, it is better to re-build the carburetor than to try to clean it out.

If you get tune-ups done at the right intervals then the carburetor should be fine.

Fuel injection systems and carburetors use two different types of fuel pumps. The right pump must be used.

Fuel injection

A dashboard light will come on when there is a problem with one of the sensors. The fuel injection system has a computer which will reveal a code. It is unnecessary to replace the whole fuel injection system if just one part is faulty. A competent mechanic who knows fuel injection systems will know how to retrieve the codes from the computer and how to troubleshoot the exact problem.

Types of fuel

Every time you pull into a gas station you see the word "octane" on the pumps. Octane is a type of chemical that is found in petroleum. The more of this chemical included in the gasoline you use the better. Think of it as the cream on top of the milk. Eighty-nine octane or 92 octane gasoline will give better performance and efficiency than 87 octane. True, higher octane gas may cost a little more on a weekly basis, but you are less likely to get engine "knock" or pinging with higher octane gas.

Pinging

Pinging is a sound like marbles rattling that you can hear when you put your foot on the gas. You could look at pinging as a sort of automobile indigestion. If you eat junk food you are likely to get heart-burn! The problem will often cure after using a few tanks of higher octane gasoline (more nutritious food).

Pinging can also be caused by too "lean" a mixture (too much air compared to fuel) or by the distributor sending the spark through at the wrong time (timing). A lot of people immediately adjust the distributor timing to handle this pinging problem but this may not be the source of the problem. Older cars were built to handle the lower octane as they used leaded gas, the lead acting as an anti-knock compound which prevented the pinging. Newer cars run at higher revolutions per minute and higher temperature in relation to the size of the engine and may require higher octane to run well.

Cleaners

Fuel injection cleaner (or carburetor cleaner) is excellent. You can occasionally add the appropriate cleaner to your gas tank when filling up, if you wish. Other fuel additives are not recommended.

If you put leaded fuel in a car that is meant to use unleaded fuel, the lead will clog up the catalytic converter. The converter is not able to burn off the lead and will cease to function properly and you will need to replace it immediately. Good luck passing your next smog test! (If there is one in your area.)

Overheating

Overheating is the worst thing that can occur to an engine. If an automobile engine were to never overheat it would probably last forever.

"Head" and "block"

An engine is said to have a "head", which consists of the upper portion containing the valve mechanisms; and an engine "block", which contains the cylinders and pistons. An engine head has to be completely air-tight and oil-tight. If there is too much pressure or too much heat the head can warp. When this occurs the engine is no longer air-tight or oil-tight. Most cars these days are made with aluminum heads which tend to overheat rather easily. When this happens the head warps and has to be re-surfaced to ensure a perfect fit where the head meets the lower engine.

Blown head gasket

The head gasket (a thin template of metal creating a seal between the upper and lower parts of the engine) will have "blown", meaning it has burnt through or warped, and will have to be replaced.

BLOWN HEAD GASKET

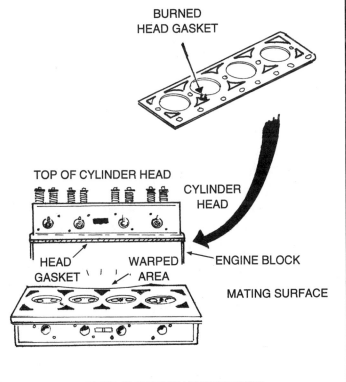

BURNED
HEAD GASKET

CYLINDER
HEAD

TOP OF CYLINDER HEAD

HEAD
GASKET

WARPED
AREA

ENGINE BLOCK

MATING SURFACE

HEAD IS SHOWN UPSIDE DOWN

Water from the cooling system mixes with the oil in the engine as a result, and you can see and feel this water when you check your oil. Re-surfacing the head and replacing the head gasket is an expensive repair job due to the labor required to take the engine apart and put it back together.

Cracked head

The head can also crack and in this case you need a new or rebuilt head. A new or rebuilt head will really hurt your checkbook! When you get a new car it will register and maintain a certain range on the temperature dial. If the temperature rises above that range something has gone wrong and you need to get it checked.

Timing problems

As we have discussed earlier, "timing" is the relationship in time between the spark, the opening of the intake valve and the compression stroke of the pistons. There is an exact relationship time-wise between the valves opening to let in gas, the pistons moving up and compressing the fuel, and the spark reaching the combustion chamber and exploding the gas. This results in smooth, efficient running of the engine. This timing is regulated by a timing mechanism in the distributor for the spark and by a belt called the timing belt for the timing of the valves and pistons.

TIMING PROBLEMS

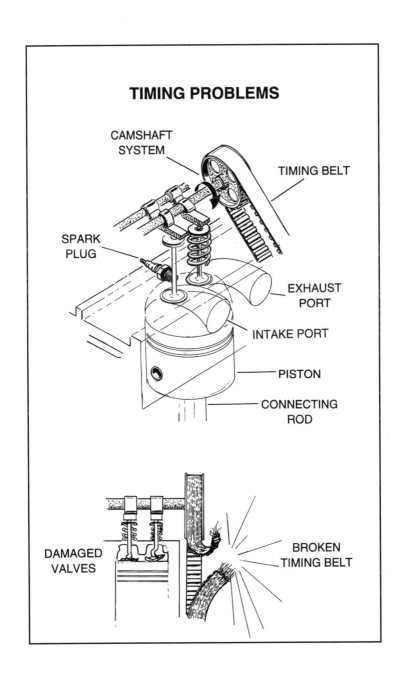

CAMSHAFT
SYSTEM

TIMING BELT

SPARK
PLUG

EXHAUST
PORT

INTAKE PORT

PISTON

CONNECTING
ROD

DAMAGED
VALVES

BROKEN
TIMING BELT

Distributor

If the timing is off at the distributor the spark will reach the combustion chamber before or after the moment when the gas is in the chamber ready to explode. The engine will run "rough" with poor power, or not at all.

Timing belt

More likely, the timing belt is incorrectly set up and the piston/valve timing is off. The explosion of gas will occur in the cylinder chamber while either the intake valve is still open or the exhaust valve is still open. This can result in a loss of power and can cause "back-firing": the fire created in the cylinder is mis-timed and instead of generating power to the crankshaft the explosion goes out through the exhaust system causing a loud bang. If the timing is out the engine can end up needing a valve job, involving replacement of the valve or valve parts, as the pressure wears them down.

Valve adjustment

Additionally the valves have to be correctly adjusted to exact specifications which vary from automobile to automobile. The opening and closing of the valves is regulated by the tappets. There is an exact clearance specified in your car manual for the correct distance between the valves and the tappets.

If you can hear the tappets then the valve clearance needs to be adjusted. If the clearance is wrong the opening of the valves will not coordinate correctly with the pistons and the spark.

Problem Valves and Pistons

Compression

The cylinders should maintain a certain level of "compression." Compression is simply a measure of the degree of "vacuum" or air-tightness in the engine. A compression test can be done to measure the amount of pressure in the combustion chamber. When you have an airtight combustion chamber you should have approximately 140 to 150 lbs. per square inch of pressure with the engine running. If the compression is bad then something is causing a leak, resulting in a lack of vacuum. The vacuum pressure is vital for the engine to work properly.

Piston rings

Piston rings are big round springs that go around the pistons and seal them off. The purpose of the piston rings is to prevent the gases from the cylinder explosion from going into the engine. Piston rings are designed to allow a minute amount of oil through for lubrication and so do not completely stop the gases from going by. Therefore it is normal for a very small amount of the carbon gas from the explosion to go by the rings. However, too much carbon can get in the pistons.

Major reason for dirty oil

Remember oil is sent all over the engine to lubricate the moving parts. Therefore it is also normal to get a little bit of carbon in your oil, the oil picking up the carbon from the cylinder as it splashes by to lubricate the side of the cylinder. (This is a major reason oil gets dirty and has to be replaced).

Blue smoke

If the valve mechanisms are leaking, (meaning they are no longer creating an air-tight compression), or if the piston rings are leaking (again no longer creating a vacuum), blue smoke will come out of the exhaust, and can be seen coming out of the tail pipe. Oil is getting inside the pistons and when it explodes it is burning the oil as well as the gasoline and air mixture.

"Blow-by"

If you have bad rings you will get what is called "blow-by." Every time the fuel/air mixture gets ignited it "blows-by" the pistons and gets into the engine. If you take your engine cap off it will blow out smoke from this "blow-by." There is a vent in the valve cover. If this puffs out continuous smoke your rings are worn.

Sometimes the rings overheat and break. The piston rings can weld to the sides of the pistons. A piston itself can break and if so it can "throw a rod" (meaning the rod connected to the pistons will destroy the crankshaft or blast a hole in the engine, requiring a new engine). Also the cylinders themselves can just wear down.

What happened?

What has occurred in all these cases is that you did not get the tune-ups that your car needed, and as a result you have wear and breakage of key engine components. It is a case of false economy or failure to take proper care of the car at the proper time.

If a car is using a lot of oil you have one of two situations to handle at once:

1. Oil is leaking out of the engine. The engine is sealed off. However, the seals are made of rubber and they do wear and let oil through. If a seal to the outside of the engine is leaking then you will get oil leaking outside the car. The oil can be seen on the outside of the engine or on your driveway.

2. You have a leaking seal inside the engine. The lubrication system is designed to move the oil around to the parts that need it but to seal off the oil from going elsewhere. If the seals going into the valves are worn, oil trickles in between the valve

and the valve sleeve and it will then trickle down into the cylinder head and burn. If the piston rings are worn oil will get sucked out of the engine and into the cavities of the cylinder head, again getting burned.

If the car is misfiring (spluttering, running rough, stalling out, etc.,) you have a problem with the spark plugs or a cylinder. It could be bad spark plugs due to carbon build up or contamination, or they have gotten too wet. The spark plugs are just two electrodes with an arc (a gap between them and the electricity creates a spark in trying to pass). They wear down after a while which is why you have to change them regularly during tune-ups. If it isn't the spark plugs then it is an engine problem.

To summarize, engine problems can include:

> a) cooling system problems
>
> b) lubrication system problems
>
> c) bad valves or incorrect valve clearances
>
> d) bad pistons or piston rings
>
> e) a broken seal or gasket
>
> f) the timing coordination between the valves the pistons and the spark is off

g) insufficient spark

An engine in good condition will be well cooled, well lubricated, well sealed, well sparked, and well coordinated. Of course it has to be well fueled too!

The Cooling System

Cooling system problems result in overheating and engine damage if not handled at once. Overheating could be caused by:

a) a bad water pump

b) a clogged radiator

c) leaking hoses

d) a broken radiator fan

e) a bad radiator core

f) a broken thermostat

g) the radiator cap needing to be replaced

h) low coolant level

Water pumps wear out and then the coolant ceases to circulate out of the engine into the radiator where it will get cooled off.

As we have discussed radiators can clog and need to be flushed out or more likely "rodded out." The radiator core can wear out and spring a leak. You will probably need a new radiator, unless the radiator shop can re-condition yours.

Hoses are rubber. Due to age, weather, and the heat going through them radiator hoses can leak, and consequently need replacing.

For engines with an electric fan, if the fan does not turn on and if the car is at a standstill with the engine running the radiator will overheat. If the fan is broken the radiator will only cool down when the car is moving (as the cooler air hits the outside of the radiator and cools the hotter air in the radiator).

If the top radiator hose is cool or sometimes completely cold, then the thermostat is not opening to let the hot water from the engine get to the radiator so it can be cooled.

The Clutch and the Transmission

The clutch pad gets worn after a period of time and you must have the pad to grip the gears of the gear-box. The length of time that the clutch will last without having to be replaced depends on how you use it.

It is possible to adjust most clutches and some are even self-adjusting. If the gear starts to engage with the clutch pedal closer to the floor of the car than usual, the clutch probably needs adjusting.

The symptom of a broken clutch is an inability to drive in any gear no matter what you do. The

CLUTCH PROBLEMS

TACHOMETER	SPEEDOMETER

IF A CLUTCH DISC IS WORN,
THE RPMs OF THE ENGINE MAY BE HIGH
FOR THE ACTUAL SPEED OF THE CAR.

plates are slipping. You can tell when the clutch is starting to go bad; you put your foot on the accelerator as you let out the clutch and the RPMs (the revolutions per minute) of the engine increase but without any forward motion; then all of a sudden the clutch starts to grip and the car starts moving.

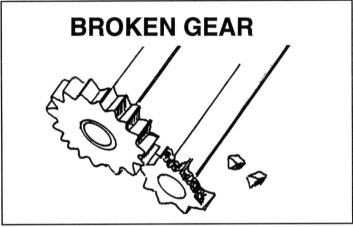

BROKEN GEAR

It's time to change your clutch before any further damage can occur or larger problems develop in your transmission system.

"Hydraulic" simply means that fluids or gases are used to create pressure and thus motion. If you can't get into gear and your car has a hydraulic clutch, then the hydraulic valves are not working or they are leaking and there is a problem with fluid in the hydraulics.

If the clutch on a car checks out okay, but you can't get into gear, then you have selector problems; meaning that your gear-box is unable to select the gears properly. Gears can get worn or broken teeth and cease to mesh and turn.

When the transmission makes a whirring sound no matter what gear you are in and there is a constant whine from underneath the car (where the transmission is located) it is time to get the transmission checked. If you hear a lot of crunching and grinding get the transmission checked out.

Get your gear box regularly checked at the same time as you get your oil changed. Check the oils in the gear-box and keep these maintained and it will last for ever. The only time a manual gear box goes bad is if it runs out of oil. In a manual transmission the gear box is sealed so you will need to get the level checked by a mechanic.

In an automatic you can check the transmission fluid level and should as part of your maintenance routine.

Whether manual or automatic the fluid should be changed annually by your mechanic. In an automatic transmission the clutches are part of the automatic gear box and when the clutches go bad the automatic transmission needs to be re-built or replaced. Because of this automatic transmissions are far more likely to need replacement than a manual gear box. When buying a second hand car this is very important to keep in mind. Replacing the transmission is an expensive repair job.

The steering system

The following difficulties could develop with the steering system:

a) the tires are worn

b) the wheels are out of balance

c) the wheel bearings have gone

d) the front end has gone out of alignment

e) something is wrong with the steering
        column

f) the joints connecting the steering
        mechanisms are worn

g) the steering box mechanism is faulty

h) the shocks are bad

i) the car frame is cracked

Tires

Check the tires regularly. In a front wheel drive car the front tires tend to wear out faster than the back. In a rear wheel drive car the back wheels will wear out first. Rotate the tires for even wear by exchanging the front tires with the back tires. Never rotate radial tires side to side. Make sure that the tires that have gotten more wear are still safe to drive. If the tires are too worn replace them.

If the car veers from side to side, then the tires are worn, the wheels are out of balance, or the front end is out of alignment. If the car shakes when driving especially at high speeds then it is the tires, or bad shocks.

Alignment

Front end alignment can be thrown off by hitting the curb or a pothole. There could be other factors causing the alignment to go out and you would need to find and fix that and then get a proper alignment. When the alignment has gone out it is important that you discover WHY before simply getting an alignment done.

If the steering joints are worn, the wheel bearings are bad, the frame is cracked, or a steering bar is cracked then this could affect the alignment. Only getting these items fixed and then a front end alignment will fix it, not an alignment alone.

If correcting tires, balance, and alignment doesn't handle a steering problem then you need to check into each of the other possibilities and fix them as a priority. It is dangerous to drive with a bad steering column, worn joints, if the rack and pinion mechanism is faulty, or the car frame is cracked. Shocks, if too "shot", can also be dangerous.

Braking system

Bad brakes will also affect the steering when braking. Brake pads wear down slowly. They are padding against the friction that occurs when the brakes grab the brake disc or drum while the car is moving. The friction burns off some of the pad. If the brake pad wears down too much then metal hits metal. When this occurs, with the friction and heat generated in applying the brakes, the brake rotors, the shoes, the discs, the calipers, and the seals are liable to melt and warp and any or all of these will need to be replaced.

Brake rotor

If when you are braking at a certain speed the steering wheel begins to shake violently your brake rotor has warped. People who live on hills have their foot constantly on the brakes when driving down the hill especially in a car with automatic transmission. The brakes go red hot and start to warp, bend, and melt. The brake rotor, because it is now warped, will grab the axle at some points and not at others as it turns. Hence the shuddering effect.

Brake fluid

You need to check the brake fluid level regularly. As a word of caution when replacing the brake

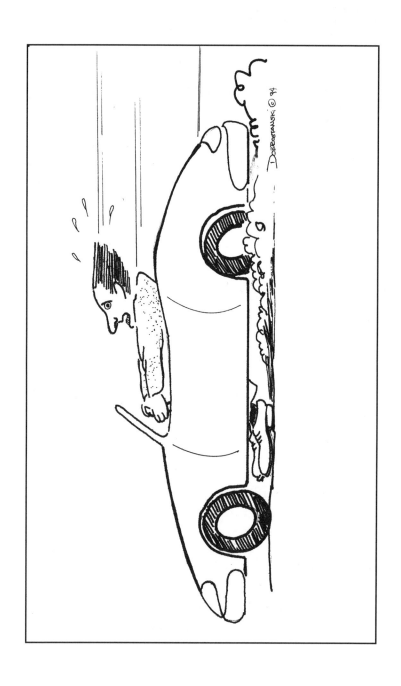

fluid in the master cylinder, don't let the fluid touch any part of your car paint. It is a chemical and will burn the paint off. If you get some on the paint by accident wash it down with water immediately.

Get your brakes checked regularly (every time you get an oil change), before there is any problem and you have added expense. **If you hear any noise coming from your brakes, if you experience any shudder when applying the brakes or if you feel the brakes getting less powerful in any way then get them checked immediately for your safety, that of your passengers and the safety of your fellow drivers.** When you get the brakes changed make sure the brake rotors are re-surfaced (this is called "turning the rotors").

Suspension system

The suspension system consists of shocks and springs and both of these can wear out, as well as the mountings that hold the shocks in place, especially in older cars.

The oil or gas in the shock valve can leak and the shocks will lose their ability to absorb and will need to be replaced. You can test the shocks to see if they are working by pushing down on one of the front corners of your car. The car should move quickly downwards and then slowly back up. If it bounces a lot when you do this then you have poor shocks. Of course you will feel it also in the quality of the ride that you get. The metal springs themselves can also break and require replacement.

The shock absorbers are also very important in protecting the mechanical parts of the car from shock. In terms of safety it is dangerous to have poor shocks. If the shocks are gone you will have reduced control over the steering of the car especially at high speeds.

PART III - BUYING YOUR CAR

CHAPTER 20. PURCHASING A CAR

There are three main factors to consider in purchasing a car, whether new or secondhand:

1. **Cost.** This includes the cost of purchase, cost of repairs, maintenance, gas consumption, insurance, and registration. For example, you may find an older eight-cylinder American car for a bargain, but the expense of running and repairing it may be exorbitant. Insurance costs will go up for a sports car or performance car. So when considering cost, figure out all of these categories of expense.

2. **Reliability.** Does it run well? Will it continue to run well? If you buy a new car and properly service and maintain it from the start, you are likely to have a trouble free automobile. If you are purchasing a used car, you have to consider how the car has been treated and its service history, and thus estimate its expected future.

3. **Features.** This is a matter of personal choice and what the bank account will bear. Do you have to have air conditioning, a radio, seats that adjust twelve ways to Sunday?

Before you start looking for your car, pre-select your requirements based on the above categories. List cost, reliability, and features that suit you best. You may have a preference for a particular make or model of car. You may have heard that cars made in such-and-such a country are more reliable, or you may have a principle of only buying American. While some cars may be made of tougher metals or heavier-duty parts than others and certain makes of car have earned a reputation over the years, beware of believing all you hear. The bottom line is how well the car has been treated and maintained.

The main sources of purchase for a used car are dealers, newspaper ads, auctions, and friends. Dealers, while likely to be a little more expensive, may give a limited warranty and stand behind the product, as they have a reputation to keep up. Auctions can be a very inexpensive way to go, or a very expensive one, depending on what you buy. Most auctions let you start the car up and listen to the engine, but you cannot drive the car around. Some auctions are open to the general public and some only to dealers. Some dealers offer a service where they will take you to an auction with them, let you choose the car to buy, inspect it as best they can, and buy it on your behalf, for a fee. Friends will usually give you a good deal, but they may not be aware of problems the car has, so check it out thoroughly regardless. Many used car purchases are done through newspaper ads. Utilize the checklist that follows and you should end up with a fair deal for yourself. Some mechanics or national road service organizations offer a service where they will check out the mechanical condition of a car you are considering buying, for a small fee.

Auto Purchasing Checklist

Use this checklist to evaluate the car you are looking at. By the noting a "yes" or a "no" on each point, by the end of the checklist, if not before, you will be able to clearly evaluate "to buy or not to buy?"

1. Call the seller on the phone and ask:

Why are you selling the car?

What is the mileage on the car?

How is it running?

Have you had any problems with the car?

What has been fixed in the last year?

Use these questions to size up the seller. Does he sound honest? Does he hem and hah? If a lot of things have been fixed recently then it is likely the car is falling apart and the seller is dumping it before he spends more money fixing it, though it may also be that everything has now been fixed and you can pick up a bargain. The character of the seller has a lot to do with it.

2. Decide to pursue this car?   yes   no

If you decide to pursue this one further, set up an appointment to see the car. Give yourself time to check the car out thoroughly. Size up the seller when you meet him/her in person.

3. Good impression of the seller? yes   no

4. Good impression of car?   yes   no

5. Maintenance records okay?   yes   no

Ask to see the repair and maintenance records. Does the seller have the manual? When was the oil last changed? If the records and manual are missing and the oil was changed 10,000 miles ago, then you have a car that has not been well taken care of and is more likely to give you trouble.

6. Owner has owner's manual?   yes   no

7. Oil changes okay?   yes   no

8. Rust okay?   yes   no

Check out the body for rust and damage.

9. Accident free?   yes   no

Is there any evidence of the car having been in an accident? Sometimes a re-done paint job can cover up accident damage. Look under the car for rust and accident evidence.

10. Leak free under car?   yes   no

Check for evidence of oil or other leaks under the car.

11. Under hood okay?   yes   no

Open up the hood. Does the engine look reasonably clean? Or is it really messy? Too dirty and it may be neglected. Too clean and it may have been steam cleaned for show, misdirecting attention away from other problems.

12. Coolant okay?   yes   no

Open the radiator cap. Is oil floating in the coolant? Does it look rusty? Both of these are bad signs.

13. Transmission/brake fluid okay?yes   no

Is the transmission/brake fluid dirty?

Have the seller start up the car while you stand over the hood and watch and listen:

14. Car starts at once?   yes   no

15. Exhaust okay?   yes   no

Does black or blue smoke blow out the exhaust? It shouldn't.

16. Engine sound smooth?   yes   no

17. Shake free?   yes   no

Does the engine shake when idling? Bad sign but it could just need a tune-up.

18. Ping/knock free?   yes   no

Have the seller step on the gas with the car in neutral. How does it sound? Any pinging or knocking noises?

19. Did the car turn off at once?   yes   no

The engine should stop at once when the key is turned off.

20. Gears clank/clash free?   yes   no

Put the car in first gear and slowly bring the clutch up if it is a manual transmission. Does the clutch engage too close to or too far from the floor? (It should engage somewhere in the middle).

21. Clutch engages okay in first gear?yes no

22. Clutch engages okay in reverse? yes no

It should engage smoothly, not jerkily for both forward and reverse. Move the car back and forth a few times. Any clanks in the transmission or strange engine noises?

23. Steering play is okay?   yes   no

Not too tight, not too loose?

24. Hand-brake works okay?   yes   no

25. Slowly drive around the block. Do the following feel and sound okay?

Engine	yes	no
Transmission	yes	no
Clutch	yes	no
Brakes	yes	no
Comfort of the ride	yes	no
Steering	yes	no

26. Take the car up to 55 MPH on the freeway. Do the following feel and sound okay?

Engine	yes	no
Transmission	yes	no
Clutch	yes	no
Brakes	yes	no
Comfort of the ride	yes	no
Steering	yes	no

27. Does the car veer:

> when you take your hands off the steering wheel?   yes   no

If so, this could be tires or alignment.

> when you brake?   yes   no

> when you hit a bump?   yes   no

Could be a suspension problem.

28. No noises when braking?   yes   no

29. No noises when changing gears? yes   no

30. Temperature looks okay?   yes   no

Watch for any indicators of overheating.

31. Other gauges okay?   yes   no

32. Lights all okay?   yes   no

Check all the lights including the brake lights, indicators, and reverse.

33. Suspension okay?   yes   no

If you push down hard on the corners of the car, does it bounce a lot? If so, you have a suspension problem.

34. Tires okay?   yes   no

Any signs of wear or unusual wear patterns could be alignment or suspension trouble.

35. Under the hood still looks okay? yes no

Check under the hood again. Any fresh oil visible after your test drive?

36. Odometer okay?   yes   no

All the numbers should line up perfectly. Does the mileage seem appropriate for the condition of the car? If not, the odometer may have been tampered with.

37. Seat belts okay?   yes   no

38. Estimated cost of needed repairs accept-
able?   yes   no

39. Features as desired?   yes   no

40. Price okay?   yes   no

41. Insurance cost okay?   yes   no

42. Want to buy it?   yes   no

By now you will have a fair picture of the car's condition. If you are still interested it is negotiation time. The factors involved in negotiating include what the buyer and seller each feel the car is worth and how badly each wants to or needs to buy or sell, versus how long the buyer is willing to shop around, and how long the seller is willing to hold out for a better price.

Get hold of the *Kelly Blue Book* which contains the range of prices at which various makes, models, and years of cars are being sold and bought on the open market.

As a rule of thumb in negotiating, a seller will often ask for more than he is willing to settle for, and the buyer will often offer less than he is willing to end up paying. The best policy is honesty and fairness. Pay a fair value if you are buying. Be honest about the condition of the car if you are selling.

Purchasing a new car:

We are not going to go into great detail about buying new cars, but when you purchase a new car there are certain factors you need to consider and certain things you need to know:

1. There is a considerable mark-up placed on the price of a new car by the dealership. The price is almost always negotiable. There are several books on the market about how to negotiate the best price on a new car. Remember to include the service and reliability of the dealership in your computation of where to buy your car.

2. Should you buy or lease your new car? The advantages of leasing are certain tax advantages and you should check with your accountant as to how these will apply to you. Leasing a car usually requires impeccable credit, much harder to get than if you are buying a car, often because you can get into a lease for next to nothing down, whereas most car loans for purchasing require you to put 20% or more down. The cost per month for a lease is often less than the monthly payments on a car purchase loan payment. However after two, three, four, or five years the lease comes to an end and the car belongs to the dealership or the bank and not to you, unless you pay an often astronomical price to retain the vehicle, usually requiring a large lump sum. Also on a lease there is usually a maximum mileage allowed

and if you go over the allotted amount (about ten to fifteen thousand miles per year average over the life of the lease) then you have a fat additional payment due. If you like to keep a car for two or three years and then get a new one, or if you can take advantage of the tax benefits, then leasing may be the hassle free and economical route for you.

3. There are certain "hidden" costs when buying a new car. If you are purchasing on a loan or lease, then you will be required by the bank that is financing you to purchase full comprehensive insurance coverage. In some states, depending on the car you get, this can be very expensive. Compare this to a used car, for which you can purchase liability and uninsured motorist coverage for quite a bit less, if you paid for the car outright. (Uninsured motorist insurance guarantees that your insurance company will pay for the damage if another motorist who is not insured is responsible for an accident that causes damage to your car, you, or your passengers). Another hidden cost is the amount you will be required to pay for your annual registration fee. This fee, in most places, is calculated based on the purchase price of your vehicle and reduces gradually year to year. If you buy a new car with a high price tag your registration will continue to be quite expensive for many years to come. Another cost to consider on a luxury car is whether it falls into the luxury tax bracket. Automobile purchases over a certain ceiling are subject to a heavy luxury tax. Again check with your accountant for the details.

4. One of the greatest advantages of a new car (if you know how to break in a new car and do so properly) is that you know the car has been handled right from the word go. The initial break-in period is crucial to the longevity of a car and if you buy a used car you can never be sure how exactly the car was treated from the start.

On the other hand if you apply the data in this book, if you choose a used car well, and ensure it is properly overhauled by a competent mechanic, then the amount you will save over the costs of a new car will cover plenty of repairs should you ever need them.

PART IV - GETTING YOUR CAR FIXED

Chapter 21. Finding a Mechanic You Can Trust

What criteria can you use to judge if a mechanic is one with whom you should do business? Let's first look at the ideal mechanic:

1. He will have a full and complete understanding of how cars work. This you can tell by his competence, his certainty, and the validity of his perceptions as borne out by excellent and rapid service.

2. He has sufficient experience with cars and how they should be that he can quickly diagnose what is wrong.

3. He knows when the error found has a more basic cause and how to trace that down.

4. He cares enough about his customers to go to the extra trouble needed in such a case and get to the real root of the problem.

5. He knows when he has found the real reason why there is a problem and handles it fully.

6. When he takes care of something it is rare that the problem will recur.

7. He respects his customer's hard earned money and doesn't perform unnecessary repairs.

8. When a customer comes in with a particular problem he takes the time to check and ensure there is nothing else that could cause trouble.

9. He gets the customer's approval before going ahead with the work.

10. He is pleasant and courteous, even when busy and harried.

11. He communicates, informing the customer of what is wrong and why, and considers it important that the customer understands.

12. He gets things done, and rapidly.

13. He keeps his shop in reasonable order and cleanliness, free of chaos.

14. If he makes a mistake he will let you know and take responsibility to correct it out of professional pride.

How does your mechanic measure up to our ideal? If you believe the majority of these points describe your mechanic then you have a jewel. If a large number of these points are violated then you may wish to look elsewhere. Talk to your friends and neighbors, to people you trust. Do they recommend a mechanic? Look around your neighborhood; talk to the mechanics and find one you feel fits the bill. Once found, there is a way to get the most out of your mechanic.

It starts with COMMUNICATION. Communication has to go both ways. A good mechanic will explain to his customers what the problem is and show them. He will explain why he needs to do what he plans to do to your car. He can show you on the diagnostic computer in many cases. He will keep the old parts that he removes and show you what was wrong with them. The mechanic has a responsibility to be ethical and honest in his business and to keep his customers informed The customer has the responsibility to treat his mechanic as a professional with the courtesy and manners that a professional deserves. Do not assume that all mechanics are crooks. Some are. Many are not. You have the responsibility to find a mechanic that you can trust.

The customer needs to get himself educated so he can clearly tell the mechanic what symptoms he has noticed and thus help the mechanic to correctly diagnose the problem. Don't expect your mechanic to be clairvoyant. If you think a mechanic may have made a mistake, then talk to him about it in a civilized manner. You may not have a full understanding of the situation and if he is not at fault and you show up raging then he can make life very difficult for you. Talk to him and find out the facts. In most cases if he has made a mistake he will do his best to rectify it. A good example is one customer with a bad transmission. This was fixed. She came screaming back to her mechanic a couple of days later that her transmission was bad again and she needed another new one. The mechanic was able to calm her down enough to get her to bring in the car. He took it for a test drive and discovered the problem was that the brakes were bad and making noise. He fixed the brakes. The customer thought she shouldn't have to pay because this was part of the transmission she had already paid for. Obviously no-one who has read this book is going to make that kind of mistake, but realize that you still may have more to learn about cars.

Never tell the mechanic what you think the problem is or that you think you need a part replaced or repaired. Let him diagnose the problem for you, and don't tempt him to repair things that may not be the problem. Remember, it is your car and in the final analysis how well it runs depends to a large degree on how you treat it and take car of it.

Here is a list of DO's and DONT's that should help to foster the best possible relations with your mechanic and get him bending over backwards for you.

DO:

1. Find yourself a mechanic that you like and that you feel is trustworthy.

2. Treat him with the respect deserved by a professional.

3. Educate yourself about cars so that you can accurately relay information and describe the symptoms occurring so as to help in a correct diagnosis.

4. Get a written diagnosis and estimate. Test drive the car before you sign off and pay for the work.

5. Understand what has gone wrong with your car and why. Get your mechanic to explain it to you if needed. Have the mechanic keep all parts removed and show you what is worn. Have him show you all the new parts. Do they look new?

6. If you think a mistake has been made, find out before making hasty accusations.

7. If you find your mechanic has been unethical get another one right away.

8. Acknowledge your mechanic for a job well done. Be loyal to a good mechanic and refer him more customers.

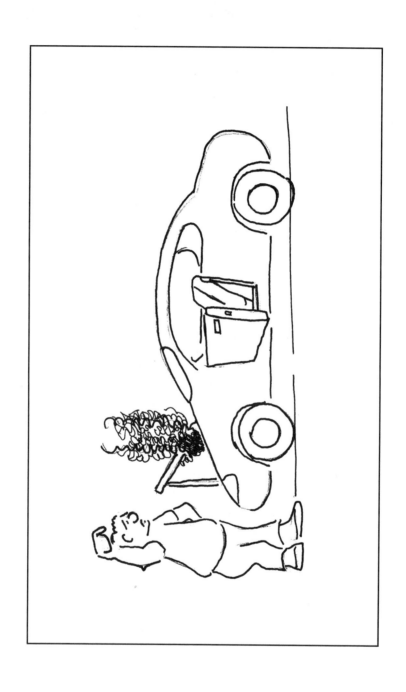

9. Realize that the state of your car is your responsibility.

10. Take good care of your car, get it properly serviced and maintained.

DON'T:

1. Assume all mechanics are crooks.

2. Go to a mechanic that you don't like or you don't trust.

3. Tell your mechanic what you think is wrong with the car.

4. Try to get free service out of your mechanic.

5. Act mean and nasty to mechanics.

6. Make out that you know more about cars than you do.

7. Blame a mechanic for the state of your car.

8. Jump down his throat if you think a mechanic made a mistake.

9. Act mean and nasty to your car, neglecting to service it.

10. Refuse to pay the bill for services rendered, when the mechanic has done the work.

Here's to a happy relationship with your mechanic!

Chapter 22. How to Avoid and Handle Rip-offs:

We have looked at the ethical mechanic. Now it is time to investigate the unethical auto repair man. Probably in many cases there are aspects of the subject of auto mechanics (basic terms and actions) that they do not understand, so they get lousy results. Desperate for business (their reputation precedes them), their concept of professional ethics goes out the window. Maybe they have incorrect concepts about how cars work and what can go wrong with them (and they need to read this book). Perhaps there are aspects of running a business itself they do not understand, such as promotion and marketing and customer service and so they are desperate to make a buck. No doubt in some cases they are just criminal, believing it is perfectly okay to take something for nothing.

Regardless of the reason let's see how they operate and what the customer can do to safeguard against getting ripped off:

• As many as 90% of the scams that occur involve the pretended repair of parts that don't need to be replaced. It goes like this:

• A customer comes along who looks like they can be taken for a ride. The mechanic tells the customer that he needs a certain part replaced when in fact there is a simpler solution and the mechanic knows it. The customer agrees to the work and goes away. Instead of replacing the part, the mechanic cleans up or paints the part so it looks like new. You pay for a new part and the labor to put a new part on. This could be done with just about any part of the car.

There are two ways to fool the mechanic who is trying to fool you:

1. You always, always ask for the old part back that supposedly was replaced. In fact the correct way to do this is to ask the mechanic before he does the work to keep the part that he replaces.

2. Go through your engine and mark every single part that you can reach. Take a knife of some kind and just make a small mark that is not very visible, but will be recognizable to you. It will take you about 30 minutes to do this to the whole engine. If you get a part replaced check to see if your mark is still there.

• Another trick used by the unscrupulous is to simulate problems that don't exist. Here are some examples that we have seen or heard about.

1. The customer comes in with a car that is overheating a bit. The temperature gauge has been going up. The mechanic tells the customer that he will diagnose the problem and to come back a little

later or to call and find out the diagnosis. The mechanic puts water into the oil in the engine and turns the engine on for a few seconds. The oil will turn into a frothy milky fluid. When the water has leaked into the engine through a blown head gasket, the oil looks just like this. The customer is told they will need a new head gasket and the heads have to be resurfaced. This is several hundred dollars cost to the customer. The mechanic just drains the oil, cleans up the engine and changes the oil. Perhaps the problem was simply a bad thermostat, a need for coolant, or other minor work.

If a mechanic says your head gasket has blown there are several simple checks you can do. The head gasket keeps oil sealed into the engine and keeps water out of the engine. Water and oil don't mix. If the head gasket is blown you can:

a) check the water in the radiator to see if it feels oily,

b) check the oil in the engine to see if it has any water in it, is bubbly or foamy,

c) leave the radiator cap off and start up the engine. If the head gasket is blown the water will shoot out of the radiator.

2. On front wheel drive cars there is a flexible joint on the drive shaft that allows the wheels to turn. It is called a CV (constant velocity) joint. This joint

is kept greased by a part called the CV boot. The mechanic cuts the CV boots to make them look bad and tells the customer "better get the CV boot replaced, you could have a drive-shaft failure", and charges to overhaul the shaft and replace the CV boot.

3. If there is a brake fluid leak the brakes could fail. By pouring brake fluid over the brake calipers a leak in the brake system is simulated and the customer pays to have the whole brake system fixed.

4. Similarly pouring oil on the sides of the engine will simulate an oil leak "requiring" the replacement of seals, gaskets or other engine work that doesn't need to be done. Clean up the oil, start the engine and see if any fresh oil appears.

5. A transmission leak can be simulated by draining your transmission fluid and telling you that the transmission is leaking and has to be overhauled. You can fill up the fluid, drive the car if it is otherwise okay, and see if the fluid goes down again.

6. It is quite simple for a mechanic to short out your electrical system, by exposing a wire and touching it to another wire. Shorts can be difficult to find and you are charged long labor hours to "find" the short.

7. Loosening your oil pan will make it look like you have a major oil leak and need engine work.

8. Cutting fuel lines or crimping (bending or twisting the lines to cause a blockage) the fuel lines will simulate a problem with the fuel system.

9. Back brakes are unlikely to be seen by the customer. More than one customer has been charged for new back brakes when they only needed and only received an adjustment.

10. The engine contains a vacuum. There are various vacuum hoses that keep the vacuum maintained. One of the hoses can come off and the engine will sound awful. All that is required is to put the vacuum hose back on. Instead you are charged for a complete tune-up, or worse.

These are just a few of the tricks that occur. If you always get the parts back after replacement, if you mark all the parts under your hood, if you find a mechanic you can trust and if you apply the DO's and DONT's in handling mechanics you will prevent the vast majority of such treachery. If you suspect that a trick is being pulled on you then go get a second opinion (without telling the second mechanic what the first one said). The best prevention of all is to ensure that you yourself gain a good understanding of the basics about cars. It is very hard to fool someone who knows.

CHAPTER 23. THE REVERSE REPAIR CHECKLIST

If your mechanic tells you that you need a certain part replaced or some specific work done to your car, how can you cross-check his diagnosis?

We have listed the major jobs that might need to be done on a car. Against each of these mechanical jobs we have listed the most likely symptoms that will occur and in some cases checks you can do to validate or question the diagnosis. Does your car exhibit any of these symptoms? If so the mechanic's diagnosis may well be validated. If not then he may be incorrect in his diagnosis. This does not mean there is any intent to mis-diagnose. Discuss it, if you have a long and successful working relationship with the mechanic, and ask him to explain a little further about what lead him to this diagnosis. Or get a second opinion from another mechanic. In this case do NOT tell the second mechanic what the first mechanic's diagnosis is, just ask him to look at the car and tell you what is wrong. The first mechanic may turn out to have been correct. So always handle such matters in a diplomatic manner.

Mechanic says you need to re-place the—	Symptoms you might expect	How to verify the diagnosis
Battery	When turning on ignition key you will get a click.	On diagnostic machine when electrical charge is put on battery it will sink to-wards dead on the dial and will not hold a charge.Have your mechanic show you this. Otherwise if it is a dead battery it can be recharged
Carburetor	Black smoke will be seen coming out of exhaust.	If car fails to start spray starter fluid into carbu-retor. If car now starts then carbu-retor is the likely fault although it could be an ob-stacle in the fuel line or fuel filter or fuel pump fail-ure.

Mechanic	Symptom	Diagnosis
Fuel pump	Fuel will not be getting through to carburetor. Engine won't start or dies.	Check to ensure it is not simply no gas, a blockage to fuel line or fuel filter, or a carburetor problem, before replacing fuel pump.
Starter motor	Clicks when turning the ignition key, but engine doesn't turn over, and battery is proven to be charged. Or crunching sound when motor is turned on and it doesn't catch, but then it does.	
Solenoid	Clicks when turning the ignition key, but engine doesn't turn over, and battery is proven to be charged.	By-pass the solenoid(by bridging heavy cable between the terminals of the solenoid) and go directly to the

Mechanic	Symptom	Diagnosis
		starter. If this works then the solenoid is bad. If it doesn't it is probably the starter.
Alternator	Shows under 13 volts on the voltage meter dial when "revving" the car. Battery goes dead again after charging yet battery is still chargeable. Car lights come on but fade out (this could be battery also). Alternator light comes on and gets brighter.	Have mechanic check alternator with diagnostic equipment and show you that it indicated alternator is bad. Have mechanic show you that battery is still rechargeable on his special equipment.
Distributor	The battery is fine but the distributor is not getting charge to the spark plugs. Car	Make sure the spark plugs and wires to the spark plug are still good. If so, it could be the coil, the

Mechanic	Symptom	Diagnosis
	shakes when idling and runs unevenly. Car dies for no apparent reason. (This could be a fuel line problem or out of gas.)	distributor rotors, or the distributor cap. Only replace what is actually bad.
Electronic ignition	Same symptoms as distributor.	
Radiator hoses	Hoses will be leaking (which is visible) and coolant will be leaking onto ground.	
Reverse flush radiator	Temperature is going up, no fault apparent in hoses.	
Rod out radiator	Reverse flush did not remove blockage to radiator.	

Mechanic	Symptom	Diagnosis
Rebuild or replace a bad water pump	Water pump will be making noise and probably leaking visibly.	
Radiator fan	Fan doesn't turn on when engine running and temperature goes up	This could also be a bad thermostat so get this replaced first.
Radiator	Overheating. Water is leaking out of radiator.	If radiator leak is not visible then rodding out radiator or replacing hoses and thermostat should handle the problem.
Belts	Screeching sound from under hood.	One of the belts will be clearly worn or loose on inspection. If loose may be able to tighten it. If worn must be replaced.
Pistons	Burning oil. Blue smoke	Ensure it is not valve seals or

Mechanic	Symptom	Diagnosis
	coming out of exhaust.	the piston rings.
Piston rings	Burning oil. Blue smoke and car idles roughly.	Take off the engine cap (where the oil is filled) and smoke will come out from "blow-by". Spark plugs will be completely black from carbon from the bad pistons and from oil contamination.
Valve seals	Burning oil. Blue smoke when first running in the morning, then blue smoke stops	Compression will show low compression on the cylinder with the valve leak. Check and replace valves if needed.

Mechanic	Symptom	Diagnosis
Adjust the valves	Audible tappet noise from incorrect clearance.	
Valves	Replacing seals did not handle the valve leak.	Valves will be visibly worn.
Crankshaft	There will be a loud consistent knock in engine.	It is more likely the bearings. If the crankshaft is the problem it will probably be unable to provide power to the transmission. You may be better off with a rebuilt engine.
Replace/rebore the cylinders	There will be a loud knock but only when flooring the accelerator. It is the sound of the pistons slapping against the cylinders.	

Mechanic	Symptom	Diagnosis
Timing chain	There will be a rustling and clicking noise.	The timing mechanism needs to be overhauled at certain intervals and your car manual will tell you when
Head gasket	Overheating. Oil in engine is milky/foamy.	Do a pressure test; if any cylinder tests as under 140 pounds per square inch then gasket is probably blown. Open radiator cap and top up water; turn engine over with cap off and if water shoots out head gasket is blown. Do a "leak down" test: put air into cylinders to see if it comes out of valves (bad valves) past the piston rings (bad rings)

Mechanic	Symptom	Diagnosis
		or past the head gasket (bad gasket).
Re-surface the warped head	Warping can be seen when head is taken off to re-place the head gasket.	Have mechanic show you where it is warped and show you the re-surfaced head be-fore it goes back on.
Cracked head	Can be seen when head is taken off to re-place the head gasket.	Have mechanic show you where it is cracked.
Adjust the clutch	Clutch engages too close to, or too far off, car floor	
Clutch	Slips, and trouble getting into gears	Adjustment may fix the problem or may not.
Gear box	Clutch has been checked and is	a) Needs lubrica-tion, but if still no

Mechanic	Symptom	Diagnosis
	O.K. but you can't get car into gear. Gears crunch.	good then: b) Needs overhaul, and if still no good, then: c) Needs replacement/rebuild of gear box.
Automatic transmission	Trouble getting car into gears, or clutches are slipping, or gears crunching.	a) Needs lubrication, but if still no good then: b) Needs overhaul, and if still no good, then: c) Needs replacement/ rebuild.
Worn CV-joint on the axle (front wheel drive).	Clicks when turning wheel.	Make sure it is not a wheel bearing. Have mechanic show you the worn part after replacing.

Mechanic	Symptom	Diagnosis
Broken U-joint on the axle (rear wheel drive)	Clanks when taking off and changing gears.	Make sure it is not a wheel bearing. Have mechanic show you the broken part after replacing.
Wheel bearings	Rumbles and hums and gets louder the faster you go.	Jack the wheel up and move from side to side and if there is any clanking then it is the wheel bearing.
Differential	Low constant hum, but doesn't get louder as you go faster.	Make sure it is not the wheel bearing.
Steering system(any part)	Excessive play when moving steering wheel, but no corresponding movement to wheels.	Could be any of these, check each: Steering box, steering column, rack and pinion, tie rod ends, steering linkage.

Mechanic	Symptom	Diagnosis
Brakes	Grinding metal to metal and/or spongy feeling on braking car:	Check all of the following: Drums and/or shoes (drum brakes), pads, discs (disc brakes), calipers, master cylinder. Only replace what is actually worn by inspection. Have mechanic show you broken or worn parts if he replaces them.
Handbrake	Brake is on fully but it is not engaging. It is the brake or the cable.	
Engine mounting	Car shakes when engaging into gear.	Ensure it is not a gear box problem. A shaking car can also be worn or unbalanced tires.

Mechanic	Symptom	Diagnosis
Exhaust system or catalytic converter	Exhaust leak. Car won't pass smog check.	Have mechanic show you the part that had to be replaced and what is wrong with it.
Muffler	Loud or deafening noise when driving.	
Shocks	Car bounces around on the road with poor control, especially when hitting bumps. Very uncomfortable ride.	Check to make sure it is not springs or shock mountings.

GLOSSARY

This glossary contains simple definitions of many of the key terms that you will come across on the subject of cars. This is not meant to be a complete automotive dictionary but should help to keep you from falling asleep when your mechanic starts talking.

If you do come across a term that is not included in this glossary note it down and see if you can get it defined at your local library. If not then contact your dealer or ask your mechanic.

ABS stands for Anti-lock Braking System. A powerful computerized brake system that will not lock up or skid, used in luxury cars.

An **accelerator** is a pedal for controlling the speed of a motor vehicle that pushes more fuel through for the engine to burn.

An **air filter** is a fine mesh through which the air going to the carburetor is passed, separating out the dirt from the air.

An **air bag** is a bag designed to fill up with gas and open automatically in the event of an impact, to protect the driver and passengers from hitting the windshield and dashboard.

Air conditioning is a device for filtering air, controlling humidity, and lowering temperature,

An **alignment** is literally "to bring into line." A repair done on special equipment to line up all parts of the front end of a car so they are straight and correctly positioned.

An **alternator** is a generator that converts mechanical energy from the engine back into electrical current and that re-charges the battery and powers various electrical parts of the car.

Anti-freeze is a chemical fluid that resists freezing. The same fluid also resists high temperatures and is known as coolant. In cold climates it is usually known as anti-freeze, and in hot climates as coolant.

An **automatic** is a car that has a transmission that changes gears automatically depending on speed and RPMs, as opposed to a manual gear box that the driver controls directly.

An **automobile**: auto = self; mobile = moves. Literally an object that moves by itself. More exactly it is a vehicle that creates its own power and is not moved by an external force.

An **axle** is a line or pole around which something revolves. In a car it is a shaft that connects the wheels and on which the wheels turn.

Balancing is the action of equalizing the weight around a wheel so that it turns in a true circle.

A **battery** is a power pack that produces electric current.

Battery cables are large wires that attach to the posts (terminals) on your battery and send current to the parts of the car or ground the battery to the body of the car.

A **bearing** is a lubricated component connecting a shaft and some other mechanical part that allows the shaft to turn with greater ease.

Belts are bands usually made of rubber that are placed around the pulleys to various parts of the car. The pulleys either move the belts or the belts move the pulleys. One belt can be attached to two different pulleys, being moved by one and moving the other. The parts involved, being turned, now operate. The water pump, the air conditioning, the power steering, etc., operate off belts in this way.

The **block** is the lower portion of the engine that houses the cylinders and pistons.

"Blow-by": If you have bad piston rings you will get what is called "blow-by." Every time the fuel/air mixture gets ignited it "blows-by" the pistons and gets into the engine.

A **brake** is a device for slowing or stopping motion by applying friction.

A **brake caliper** is a piston that pushes against the disc (in disc brakes) making the brake work.

A **brake disc** is a disc or rotor that is attached to the axle inside the wheel and holds the brake pad.

A **brake drum** is a drum that attaches to the inside of the wheel and spins, causing the brake shoe and pad to work.

Brake fluid is a special liquid that can be compressed to create pressure that operates the brakes in a car.

Brake pads are plates that create friction when squeezed against a brake disc or shoe. They are made of metal or asbestos or a synthetic. They wear down from the friction and need replacement from time to time.

A **brake shoe** is a metal clamp that fits inside the drum of a drum brake and that clamps onto the wheel as the drum spins to slow or stop the car.

A **bumper** is a device attached to the front and back of the body of a car to absorb shock and protect the passengers and prevent damage in the event of impact.

A **cam** is a device that lifts a lifter that in turn opens up the valve. It opens and shuts a valve at the right time.

A **camshaft** is a shaft to which cams are fastened and that controls the valves in the engine.

A **carburetor** supplies an internal combustion engine with the right amounts of fuel and air mixture in a vaporized form.

A **catalytic converter** is part of the exhaust system. It burns up some of the exhaust gases before they hit the air.

Charge is a flow of electricity. To charge a battery in a car is to force electrons back into the battery, reversing the chemical process that released the electricity from the battery. In this way the battery is now ready to generate a flow of charge once again.

The **chassis** is the supporting framework to which the rest of the frame, the body, the engine, etc. are bolted.

A **choke** is a valve that decreases or shuts off ("chokes") the supply of air into the carburetor so as to make the fuel/air mixture "richer" (higher in fuel content).

A **circuit** is a completed flow of electricity. Electrical parts can only operate when the electrical flow makes a complete circuit.

A **clutch** is a disc that connects two parts of a mechanism. If one part is sending force or power to another part it is said to be "driving". The part it is driving is said to be "driven." A clutch connects or disconnects a "driving" part to a "driven" part controlling the transfer of force or power.

Coasting is the action of moving at a given rate without effort. In a car maintaining a steady speed in high gear without any real increase of pressure on the accelerator pedal is called coasting. Letting the car move while the clutch is depressed and the car is out of gear is also called coasting.

A **combustion chamber** is the chamber formed by the piston and the cylinder in a car in which the fuel/air mixture is burnt.

Compression is the action of something being squeezed. In a car engine it is pressure that can be measured when the air is squeezed out of the engine and a vacuum is created.

Coolant is another name for anti-freeze.

The **cooling system** circulates the coolant around the engine.

The **crankcase** is the case that houses the crankshaft.

The **crankshaft** is the metal shaft that goes through the engine, connecting to all the pistons, that turns at thousands of revolutions per minute. It is powered by the pistons and in turn sends power to the transmission.

A **CV-joint (constant velocity)** is a flexible joint on the drive shaft that allows the wheels to turn.

A **cylinder** is the housing into which a piston fits and in which combustion takes place.

A **defogger** is an electrical strip attached to the rear window of a car that heats up and clears away mist and fog.

Diagnostics is the art of identifying the source of a problem by its symptoms. Diagnostic machines can be employed in diagnosing certain automobile problems.

A **differential** is a gear that controls how much force is sent to each of the wheels in a car, allowing one wheel to go faster than another when needed.

A **dipstick** is any stick that is dipped into a fluid container to measure the fluid level.

A **distributor** is a device for directing current to the spark plugs of an engine.

A **distributor cap** contains the electrical "points" which generate the spark to the spark plugs. Wires (called spark plug wires) connect the distributor cap to the spark plugs.

Electricity is a flow of electrons.

Electrons are simply particles that contain a type of energy (or electrical charge) that has been named "negative charge".

Emissions are gases given off by the exhaust of a car.

Emissions testing tests the content of these emissions, determining if the catalytic converter is operating to set standards.

An **engine** is literally something that produces. In a car it produces mechanical power that is then converted into motion.

Engine capacity is the size of the engine. It is actually the measurement of the volume of the piston chambers.

Engine block: see block.

Exhaust is the poisons put out into the air by a car. It is also short for the exhaust system which is the set of devices that extracts these gases from the engine and sends them out the tail-pipe.

The **exhaust manifold** is the manifold that takes the exhaust gases from the exhaust valves and directs them into the exhaust system.

The **exhaust valve** is the valve that lets the exhaust gases out of the engine after they are burnt.

A **fan** is a device for producing a current of air. There can be several fans on a car to cool off engine parts or passengers.

The **fan belt** is the belt that puts the radiator fan into motion.

The **fly wheel** is a heavy wheel used to regulate the motion of machinery. In a car the fly wheel is connected to the starter and the crankshaft and turns the crankshaft over when the starter is switched on.

The **float** is a part of the carburetor that floats in the fuel and regulates the flow of gas into the carburetor from the gas tank.

A **fog lamp** is a special lamp designed to penetrate fog and increase visual perception during foggy weather.

A **four cylinder car** is one that has four combustion chambers lined up together to create power.

Four-stroke cycle: the explosion cycle that takes place in the engine has four stages or strokes and the pistons go through these four stages repetitively, at very high speed. The four stroke cycle takes place within each individual cylinder.

A **four-wheel drive car** is one in which power is transmitted to create driving force in both front wheels and back wheels.

Freon is a gas that is freezing cold when released into air. This gas is a component of air conditioning systems.

Front end is the front of the car. It is often used to refer to the frame, chassis, transmission, and steering components at the front of the car and their alignment.

Front wheel drive is where the transmission sends the power that drives the forward motion of the car to the front axles and wheels.

Fuel is a substance that when burnt will produce heat and energy.

Fuel injection is a computerized system for injecting the desired amount of fuel into the engine for combustion.

A **fuel filter** is a filter that cleans dirt out of the gasoline as it passes through.

The **fuel line** is the complete line through which the gasoline flows, from gas tank to carburetor.

A **fuel pump** is a mechanical device that pumps fuel from the gas tank to the carburetor.

A **fuse** is an electrical safety device, containing a metal wire or strip. When a flow of electricity is too strong the fuse melts, interrupting that circuit and preventing damage to the electrical machinery involved.

Gasoline (gas) is a flammable liquid derived from petroleum oil.

A **gasket** is a type of seal used to prevent a joint from leaking.

A **gear** is a round mechanical component with teeth. One gear connects to another gear of smaller or larger size by having teeth of the same size that fit into one another (called intermeshing). Smaller gears have less teeth and larger gears have more teeth. A gear may be attached to and receive power from, or transfer power to, a shaft.

A **gear box** is a box that houses the gears and the mechanisms that allow the gears to shift and operate.

A **gear ratio** is simply how many teeth one gear has compared to another gear that it is meshing with.

The ratio between a gear with 20 teeth to a gear with 10 teeth is 2:1.

A **gear stick** is a stick that connects to the gear box and by which the driver can control the shifting of gears up and down.

A **governor** is a gear that monitors speed and controls/governs the change of gears in an automatic transmission

A **ground** is an object that connects an electrical circuit with the earth. Any electrical circuit to function must be "grounded" in this way.

The **head** is the top portion of the engine that houses the valves.

The **head gasket** is the flexible seal that sits between the head and the block.

The **heater** is a small radiator with a fan that blows hot air into the passenger compartment from the engine compartment.

The **hood** is the metal covering over the engine compartment that lifts up.

Hoses are flexible tubes that carry fluid or air from one place to another.

Hydraulic is the utilization of pressure generated by fluids or gases to create motion in a part of a machine.

Hydraulic brakes are brakes that use fluids to assist the braking action: see power brakes.

Ignition is the action of setting fire to something. In a car it is setting fire to the fuel by using a spark.

Indicators are lights that indicate to another driver or pedestrian that you are going to move in a certain direction.

In-line refers to an engine in which all the pistons are in a straight line.

The **intake manifold** is the manifold that takes the fuel and air from the carburetor to each of the intake valves.

The **intake valve** is the valve that lets the fuel and air into the engine.

Internal combustion. An automobile comes with an engine, or motor, which burns fuel to create heat and pressure. The engine is called an "internal combustion" engine which means literally that it creates a fire and burns fuel inside the engine. ("Internal" = inside; "combustion" = burns).

A **jack** is a device for raising part of a car off the ground so as to change tires or do other repairs.

Jump start is the action of attaching a car battery that is good to a car battery that is dead and transferring a boost of electricity by means of jumper cables so as to recharge the dead battery and so get that car started.

Lower engine: see block.

A **lubricant** is a material such as grease or oil that reduces the friction between moving parts.

Lug nuts are the large nuts that hold the wheel onto the axle.

A **lug wrench** is a wrench specially made to tighten and loosen lug nuts.

Manifold: "Mani" = many and "-fold" = parts, thus manifold means literally many parts.

Manual means worked by hand.

A **manual transmission** is a transmission in which the shifting of the gears is controlled by the driver by manually moving the gear stick.

The **master cylinder** holds the brake fluid that creates the pressure to operate the brakes.

Mechanical just means "performed by a machine."

A **motor** by definition is something that creates motion.

A **muffler** is a device that deadens noise. It attaches to the exhaust pipe and reduces the noise resulting from the expulsion of the exhaust fumes.

Neutral is a position of the gear stick and the gear box where the gears are neither in drive or reverse.

Octane number (or rating) is a number representing the anti-knock properties of a gasoline. The higher the better.

An **odometer** is an instrument for measuring distance traveled and showing this on a dial. The word comes from the Greek root "hodus" meaning distance and "meter" meaning to measure.

Oil is a greasy liquid that is taken from deposits in the ground. It is used to lubricate machines and engines.

An **oil change** is the action of removing oil that is dirty and putting in fresh, clean oil.

An **oil filter** cleans dirt and impurities out of the oil.

The **oil pan** is a container at the base of the engine that holds the oil.

An **overflow** is an outlet or a container for surplus liquid.

Petrol is the British term for gasoline.

Pinging is a "ping, ping, ping" sound you can hear when you put your foot on the gas. Low octane gas may not disperse correctly and can cause the engine to ignite the gas prematurely, causing a pinging noise.

A **piston** is a plunger that moves up and down and pushes some other part (like a shaft) in the process. In the engine the piston is a short cylinder that moves up and down inside the combustion chamber cylinder, receiving and transmitting motion.

Piston displacement is the method of measuring engine size. If a piston is placed into a container of fluid it will move a certain amount of the liquid out of the way or "displace" it. The piston size is stated as being the volume of fluid so displaced.

Piston rings are big round springs that go around and seal off the pistons. The piston rings are designed to stop too much of the gases from the cylinder explosion from going into the engine.

Points are electrical connectors in the distributor cap that send the spark to the spark plug.

Power is defined as "potential motion."

Power brakes are hydraulic brakes, letting fluid through a valve to increase the pressure and thus magnifying the force that the driver applies to the brakes.

Power steering is steering that uses hydraulics to assist the driver, magnifying the force applied by the driver by using the pressure of fluids.

Power windows are electrically driven windows.

A **pulley** is a round disc with a groove in it for holding or gripping a belt. The pulley moves in a circle and it either drives or is driven by a belt.

A **pump** uses constant pressure to move fluid along channels to where it is needed.

Radial tires consists of rubber material on the outside tread circled around the tire while layers of tire beneath this are laid at right angles to the tread making a long lasting and tough tire.

A **radiator** is a device that "radiates" or that sends out heat. In a car it receives hot water or coolant that has been heated up by the engine, radiates the heat into the outside air, cooling off the water or coolant, before returning it to the engine.

A **radiator hose** is a hose that carries the water or coolant to or from the radiator.

A **radiator flush** is the action of cleaning out a radiator by flushing it through with clean water.

The **rear end** is the frame, chassis, transmission, and steering components at the back of the car and their alignment.

Rear wheel drive is where the transmission sends the power that drives the forward motion of the car to the front axles and wheels.

Reverse is a gear that turns in the opposite direction to the forward gears and allows the car to move backwards.

Revs are revolutions per minute of the crankshaft, also known as RPMs.

Rocker arm is part of the valve mechanism on an engine that works with a rocking motion.

A **rod** is a metal stick. A piston has a rod attached to it that attaches to and turns the crankshaft.

A **rotor** is something that turns. There is a rotor in the distributor that turns to distribute the spark to each spark plug in turn. The brake discs are also called rotors as they turn around the axles.

RPMs: abbreviation for revolutions per minute.

RV stands for recreational vehicle, such as a home on wheels.

SAE (on cans of oil) stands for Society of Automotive Engineers.

Sealant is a substance used to fasten seals in place.

Seals are thin strips or sheets placed where two parts meet to create a seal through which liquids or gases can neither leave or enter. A seal prevents a lubricant from escaping from a specific area where it is needed; or prevents unwanted oil, water, or other substances from entering an area where they are not wanted.

Sealed beam units are headlight units.

A **shaft** is a long piece of connecting metal often attached to a piston at one end and usually a gear at the other. It transfers power along that connection as it turns.

Shocks are devices that absorb the shocks from the road, to increase the safety and comfort of the ride.

Smog testing checks the catalytic converter to see if it is removing the required levels of poison from the exhaust gases before sending them out into the atmosphere.

A **solenoid** is a coil of wire that acts as a switch and carries electricity to the starter.

Spark plugs are small plugs that fit into the engine cylinders and carry a spark.

Springs are part of the suspension system, together with the shocks.

A **spring** is a mechanical component that holds tension and releases tension.

A **starter** is an electric motor that connects to the crankshaft of the engine and gets the motion of the crankshaft started.

Steering is the action of controlling the direction of motion.

The **steering column** is the column that transfers the motion made by the driver of the steering wheel to the axles and wheels.

A **stroke** is an up or down motion made by a piston.

A **switch** turns the power (usually electrical) on and off to a component.

The **suspension** is the combination of springs and shocks on which the car is suspended.

A **tachometer** is a device that tracks and indicates the speed of rotation, in the case of a car the speed of rotation of the crankshaft. Comes from the Greel "tachos" meaning speed and "meter" meaning to measure.

A **tappet** is literally a "little tap." It is a lever attached to the valve on one side and the cam on the other and like a tap opens or closes the valve.

A **terminal** is a device that can receive or send a flow (in the case of a car it is the flow of electricity.) The terminals are the posts at either end of the battery.

A **thermostat** is a device that tracks temperature and opens or closes a valve when the temperature goes above or below a certain level.

Throwing a rod is where the rod attached to the piston breaks off and is thrown, usually demolishing the crankshaft and tearing a hole in the side of the engine.

Timing is the coordination of fuel intake, spark, and piston motion in the engine.

The **timing belt** is the belt connecting the cam shaft and the crankshaft. It controls the coordination of timing between the piston motion and the opening and closing of the valves.

The **timing chain** is a timing belt made of metal.

A **timing light** is a light that allows you to see and so correctly coordinate the distributor position with piston #1.

Tires are rubber cushions containing compressed air that encircle the wheels.

Torque is force that is used to produce rotation. In a car the force produced in the engine rotates the crankshaft, the force transferred to the transmission rotates the drive shaft. These are examples of torque.

Transmission is the system by which power is transmitted from the engine to the wheels.

Transmission fluid is the fluid which lubricates the transmission.

A **tune up** is the action of fine tuning an engine, adjusting or replacing worn or broken parts to bring an engine back up to peak efficiency.

A **turbo** is simply a big fan that is driven by the exhaust gases. The fan pushes more air through the intake valve into the pistons. This then forces in more fuel to create a balanced air/ fuel mixture. When the engine reaches a certain speed it starts to kick in.

To **turnover** describes the action of the crankshaft revolving, especially when the engine is started.

The **trunk** is the enclosed luggage space usually at the rear of the passenger compartment, so called because it used to look like and function as an old fashioned luggage trunk. In Britain called the "boot".

A **U-joint** is a flexible joint on the drive shaft that allows the wheels to turn.

A **vacuum** is an absence of air.

A **valve** is a device that temporarily closes a passage or permits movement in one direction only. A valve opens and shuts to let fluids or gases in or out.

A **valve job** is the action of rebuilding or replacing the valves in an engine.

Viscosity is the property of a fluid that causes it to not flow or resist flowing. Oil with low viscosity will flow freely, oil of high viscosity will flow with greater difficulty. As hot weather will tend to make oil thin and flow faster, higher viscosity is preferred. As cold thickens oil, a lower viscosity is required in colder climates.

A **volt** is a measure of electrical pressure, that is how much force is behind the flow of electricity. Twelve volts just means more push of electricity than, say, 9 volts, and thus can power more devices.

The **water jacket** surrounds the engine so that the water or coolant can flow around the engine and keep it from overheating.

The **water pump** is a mechanical device for pumping water out of the engine, through the thermostat to the radiator.

WD-40 is a lubricant.

A **wheel** is a circular disc that revolves driven by a pole or axle that goes through its center.

A **wheel bearing** is a bearing that connects -*the wheel and the axle and allows for a smooth lubricated flow between the two.

The **windshield** is the glass screen through which the driver looks at the road in front and that protects him from the wind (bugs, stones, etc.). It is called a windscreen in Britain.

Window wipers are devices that can move back and forth across the windshield removing water when it is raining or when cleaning off the windshield.

INDEX

A

ABS 92
accelerator 53,
    55, 76, 78,
    79, 164
acid solution 31
air bags 98
air cleaner 38
air conditioning
    33, 98, 174
air filter 39,
    125, 140, 149
air intake 41
air valve 39
alignment 87, 88,
    118, 121, 166, 168
alternator 31, 32,
    34, 102,
    106, 130, 141,
    142, 146, 148
alternator belt
    148
anti-lock braking
    system 92
auctions 175
auto repair store
    126
automatic trans-
    mission
    68, 78, 79,
    165, 169
axle(s)56, 67, 80,
    81, 89

B

"back-firing" 156
balancing 118
ball bearings 65
battery
    22, 23, 24,
    25, 27, 29,
    31, 32, 33,
    34, 47, 102,
    105, 106, 118,
    129, 130, 131,
    132, 141, 142,
    146
battery fluid level
    118
bearing(s) 20,
    65, 66
belt 20, 50, 51,
    58
block 152
"blow-by." 158
"blows out" 144
brake(s)
    18, 74, 89,
    113, 117, 121,
    123, 169, 171,
    180, 181,190,
    199
brake calipers 199
brake disc 169
brake drum 169
brake fluid 89, 111,
    112, 113, 117,
    125, 178, 199
brake fluid level
    123, 169

brake line(s) 89,
    92
brake pads 92,169
brake pedal 89
brake rotors 169
brake "shoes" 92
brake system 199
braking power 92
braking system
    16, 89, 92,
    104, 169
break-in period
    186
buy or lease 184

C

caliper(s) 89, 92
    169
camshaft 51, 52
camshaft pulley
    52
carburetor 38
carbon monoxide
    82
carburetor(s)
    15, 37, 38,
    39, 41, 53,
    103, 105, 107,
    140, 149, 150
carburetor cleaner
    151
carburetor pump
    37
carburetor valve
    53
catalyst 82

ORDER FORM

Name _____

Address _____

City/State/Zip _____

Phone _____

Enclosed is my check for $20.45 ($16.95 for *ALL ABOUT YOUR CAR* and $3.50 for shipping).

THE TROUBLESHOOTING CHECKLIST booklet is available separately for $3.25 ($2.00 and $1.25 shipping).

DIMI PRESS
3820 Oak Hollow Lane, SE
Salem, OR 97302-4774

Phone 1-800-644-DIMI(3464) for orders
or 1-503-364-7698 for further information
or FAX to 1-503-364-9727
or by INTERNET to dickbook@aol.com

Call toll-free and order now!

OTHER DIMI PRESS PRODUCTS FOR YOU

TAPES are available for..$7.95 each

> **#1-LIVE LONGER, RELAX**
> **#2-ACTIVE RELAXATION**
> **#3-CONQUER YOUR SHYNESS**
> **#4-CONQUER YOUR DEPRESSION**
> **#5-CONQUER YOUR FEARS**
> **#6-CONQUER YOUR INSOMNIA**
> **#7-CONQUER YOUR CANCER**
> **#8-LAST LONGER, ENJOY SEX MORE**
> **#9-WEIGIIT CONTROL**
> **#10-STOP SMOKING**
> **#11-LIVE LONGER, RELAX (female voice)**
> **#12-ACTIVE RELAXATION (female voice)**
> **#13-UNWIND WHILE DRIVING**
> **#14-RELAX AWHILE**
> **#15-RELAX ON THE BEACH/MEADOW**
> **#16-HOW TO MEDITATE**

TAPE ALBUM has six cassettes and is titled:

> **GUIDE TO RELAXATION** $29.95

BOOKS

> **KOMODO, THE LIVING DRAGON (Rev. Ed.)** is the only
> account of the world's largest lizard $14.95
> **BUILD IT RIGHT!** is a book of advice on what to watch out for
> as you build your own home...$16.95
> **HOW TO FIND THOSE HIDDEN JOBS** helps job-seekers or
> career-changers in their search..$13.95
> **BRING ME A MEMORY** is a touching story of an 11-yr.-old
> girl who loses her father $9.95
> **FEEL BETTER! LIVE LONGER! RELAX** is a manual of relax
> ation techniques and a history of relaxation...........................$9.95
> **WRESTLING BACK** is a true account of an athlete and his
> mother struggling to recover from his devastating injury.......$14.95